Building a Small Business That Warren Buffett Would Love

Building a Small Business That Warren Buffett Would Love

Adam Brownlee

WILEY

John Wiley & Sons, Inc.

Published by John Wiley & Sons, Inc., Hoboken, New Jersey.
Published simultaneously in Canada.

No part of this publication may be reproduced, stored in a retrieval system, or transmitted in any form or by any means, electronic, mechanical, photocopying, recording, scanning, or otherwise, except as permitted under Section 107 or 108 of the 1976 United States Copyright Act, without either the prior written permission of the Publisher, or authorization through payment of the appropriate per-copy fee to the Copyright Clearance Center, Inc., 222 Rosewood Drive, Danvers, MA 01923, (978) 750-8400, fax (978) 646-8600, or on the Web at www.copyright.com. Requests to the Publisher for permission should be addressed to the Permissions Department, John Wiley & Sons, Inc., 111 River Street, Hoboken, NJ 07030, (201) 748-6011, fax (201) 748-6008, or online at http://www.wiley.com/go/permissions.

Limit of Liability/Disclaimer of Warranty: While the publisher and author have used their best efforts in preparing this book, they make no representations or warranties with respect to the accuracy or completeness of the contents of this book and specifically disclaim any implied warranties of merchantability or fitness for a particular purpose. No warranty may be created or extended by sales representatives or written sales materials. The advice and strategies contained herein may not be suitable for your situation. You should consult with a professional where appropriate. Neither the publisher nor author shall be liable for any loss of profit or any other commercial damages, including but not limited to special, incidental, consequential, or other damages.

For general information on our other products and services or for technical support, please contact our Customer Care Department within the United States at (800) 762-2974, outside the United States at (317) 572-3993 or fax (317) 572-4002.

Wiley also publishes its books in a variety of electronic formats. Some content that appears in print may not be available in electronic books. For more information about Wiley products, visit our web site at www.wiley.com.

Library of Congress Cataloging-in-Publication Data:

Brownlee, Adam, 1978–
    Building a small business that Warren Buffett would love / Adam Brownlee.
      p. cm.
    Includes index.
    ISBN 978-1-118-13888-5 (cloth); ISBN 978-1-118-22550-9 (ebk);
    ISBN 978-1-118-23889-9 (ebk); ISBN 978-1-118-26355-6 (ebk)
    1. Small business—Finance. 2. Investments. 3. Buffett, Warren. I. Title.
    HG4027.7B76 2012
    658'.022—dc23

                                        2011046752

10 9 8 7 6 5 4 3 2 1

To Michelle and Cooper—I love you very much.

Contents

Foreword

It is not often that you come across a book that is both timely and timeless. With the unemployment rate at record highs, there is not a better time to build a dream and create jobs through small business. If you are seeking to start a small business or currently in small business, then follow the guidelines laid forth in *Building a Small Business That Warren Buffett Would Love* in order to build a business with rock solid fundamentals. As pointed out in the text, why build a business on loosely knitted frameworks or second-hand guess work when the principles of the world's greatest investor are available? This is the protocol that Warren Buffett has used to identify great businesses to invest in, so why not start there? Why not inject this mold into the center of your business and build an outstanding business from the inside out, one that has a greater chance of success, one that can provide a living, one that can fulfill a dream and one that Warren Buffett would love.

DANIEL TICHENOR, *CAGE THE ELEPHANT*

Acknowledgments

I would like to thank the staff at John Wiley & Sons for their efforts and support in truly making this a success. I would like to thank Becky Naugle and the entire staff of the Kentucky Small Business Development Centers, one of the finest business service providers in the country. Much appreciation goes to Neal Scott, Tamara Ward and Marcus Lemonis for building a living, breathing business that Warren Buffett would love, Camping World. I would also like to thank President Gary Ransdell of Western Kentucky University for his enduring leadership. Finally, I would like to thank my family and especially my wife for her unwavering support.

A.B.

Building a Small Business That Warren Buffett Would Love

Introduction: Painting the Picture of the Ideal Business

Someone is sitting in the shade today because someone planted a tree a long time ago.
—Warren Buffett

Ah, but I was so much older then, I'm younger than that now.
—Bob Dylan

They're Gr-r-reat!

—Tony the Tiger, mascot of a consumer monopoly company that Warren Buffett loves

A consistent truth exists across all small businesses: Each one is different. A hamburger stand drives down operational costs through inexpensive, rapid-fire delivery; a service business builds sustainability through solid, enduring relationships; a technology firm evolves through bleeding-edge innovation and development. It would be catastrophic for a tax service provider to ram his clients through in 60 seconds just as it would be suicide for a hamburger stand cashier to play a round of golf with customers as the drive-thru line backs up. No matter how disparate the business model universe may be, another consistent truth exists: Every great business is built upon the same core fundamentals.

1

There Is a Template

The core of a strong business is not a mystery, nor is it a complicated mess. It is found in the wisdom of Warren Buffett, which is a virtual blueprint to create superior business results and build a powerful small business engine. If you follow this blueprint, digest its meaning, and learn its intricacies, you can build an economically superior small business, one that Warren Buffett would love.

You Hold in Your Hands the Blueprint

If you asked Warren Buffett what he looks for in great business, this is what he would say:

- I want to see a consumer monopoly . . .
- With a strong track record of earnings.
- With a healthy return on equity.
- With the ability to reinvest those earnings at a high rate of return.
- With little or no debt on the balance sheet.
- With the ability to increase prices with inflation.
- With a healthy net and gross margin relative to other businesses and industries.[1]

These statements embody the principles that Warren Buffett used to turn an initial $105,000 investment into a $40 billion fortune; and if the principles are wielded appropriately, they can be used to transform a small business into an economic powerhouse. This, folks, is our road map.

The Context—Focus on the Fundamentals First

Instead of hacking at the proverbial leaves of a bad business—a missing marketing plan, anemic revenues, low inventory turnover—let us first examine for cancer at the root via the Buffett principles. If a tumor is found, let us determine if intense fundamental therapy as prescribed in the following chapters can save the business, and if not, then it is time to move to higher ground and seek out a better business model. Remember, parameters such as return on equity, and debt to equity allow us to compare across multiple business models. If the current business is terminally ill after delivering year after year of poor returns, then it is time to take a bold step.

Let us first check that we are in the right forest before cutting down the trees.

Who Says? Warren Buffett Does

Don't take my word for it; take Warren Buffet's. I could affront you with a spaghetti tapestry of professional credentials but why bother? Warren Buffett is available and his track record is much more stupendous than mine. He grew his initial investment of $105,000 into a $40 billion fortune over 40 years.[2] I cut my grass yesterday.

Let us start at the fundamental fountainhead as prescribed by Mr. Buffett before moving onto tactical measures such as forecasting financial statements or business plan development. Let us build a small business that Warren Buffett would love.

It Is Easier Said than Done—A Preview

Regarding Buffett's second principle, "*with a strong track record of earnings*": It is painfully obvious that a healthy business needs a strong track record of earnings in order to be viable. A business without earnings, which represent everything left over on the income statement after all expenses—cost of goods sold, payroll, utilities, taxes, and so on—have taken their bite, is like a lawn mower without a lawn mower blade. It may be fun to circle the yard a few times, but after a while the grass needs cutting. A for-profit business is "in business" to generate earnings, which in turn, when divided by the initial investment or equity, leads to a return. The bottom line on the income statement—earnings—represents the pulse of a business, and Buffett seeks out strong, steady 10-year earnings track records. The entrepreneur should strive to generate strong earnings track records. If this is not a priority, then perhaps your time is better spent circling the yard on a bladeless lawn mower.

Earnings lead to another empirical Buffett fundamental rule, return on equity. Return on equity can be thought of as the common size ratio used to illustrate the productivity of the equity in the business and can be used for comparison purposes. Think of it this way: If you put premium gas (equity) in a jalopy (business), the overall performance of the car will be poor, regardless of the gasoline grade. If on the other hand you put the gas in a new Corvette, all things equal, the car performance should be much better. (You can hug corners, get stuck on speed bumps.) Return on equity is used to distinguish a business jalopy from a Corvette, and is found simply by dividing earnings by the amount of invested equity.

For example, a fourplex generating $10,000 in yearly earnings, with $100,000 of invested equity, is producing a 10 percent return on equity ($10,000/$100,000). This rate of return is superior to a CD at the local bank that is coming in at 4 percent.

In the context of cash flow and financial independence, the smaller the return the greater the capital needed. For example, at a rate of return of 5 percent and monthly expenses of $3,000, it will take $720,000 of investment capital in order to generate $3,000 per month and be financially independent. At a rate of return of 10 percent, the required investment is only $360,000. Quite a difference . . . like half!

A Business Plan Is Written Once

Remember this also: A business plan is typically written once, but fundamentals are timeless and diamonds are forever. Sure, it is necessary to revise and update the business plan as economic conditions and business strategies dictate, but accurate business coordinates on a compass, as found in the investment principles of Warren Buffett, again are timeless. Let us first build this rock solid framework before adjusting the nuts and bolts.

Bad Pizza Joint . . . Bad

I have worked with numerous struggling businesses lacking solid underlying fundamentals that could use a healthy dose of Buffett. Case in point: I recently met with the owner of a local pizzeria whose business has very little differentiation from the local mega chains. Net, net, his operation is embroiled in head to head competition with the likes of Domino's and Pizza Hut. The owner of the small shop works night and day and is very passionate about his business. Still, over the past five years, Domino's has spent an estimated $1.4 billion in national advertising in the United States.[3] Although I am always fond of the underdog and tend to root for him, this is just one battle the small guy cannot win—at least not on this battlefield.

What he can do, in following our plan to build a business that Warren Buffet would love, is create consumer-monopoly differentiation and distinguish his business from the mega chains. Currently his model is very similar to the delivered, standard quality pizza of

Domino's. For our small guy, this results in head-to-head failure. Even loyal fans will eventually capitulate, making the switch based on Domino's systematized, superior delivery framework with its built-in, machete price slicing offers. As it stands, our pizza guy does not have a chance (Mama Mia!) and must differentiate his model lest he sits stagnant in a slowly spiraling vortex of death. Perhaps he can implement a Hawaiian luau theme complete with a tomato sauce-spewing volcano that erupts every hour on the hour. An Elvis impersonator can perform a couple of numbers (Live! Via Satellite!) before gorging himself on a fried peanut butter and banana pizza just to show the customers how good it is.

I kid a little, of course, but this concept is founded on the same consumer monopoly concept that Warren Buffett loves to see in a business. Coke is Coke because the company has built up an enduring consumer brand over the past 120 years, and if the cans, bottles, and two liters disappeared off the shelves of the local supermarket warehouse tomorrow, most people would take note. The same can be said for the local Hawaiian themed pizza shop that spews pizza sauce every hour while a fat guy in a jumpsuit obliterates a Chicago pan to the tune of *See See Rider*. If that went away, customers would notice.

How to Paint

We have a road map courtesy of Warren Buffett, but what do we do with it? How can we take the principles of a consumer monopoly, with a strong track record of earnings, a healthy return on equity, with the ability to reinvest the earnings at a high rate of return, with little or no debt on the balance sheet, the ability to increase prices with inflation, and a healthy net and gross margin relative to other businesses and industries, and wire it into a small business in order to build a small business that Warren Buffett would love?

First we take a step forward, and then backward, and now we are cha-cha-ing!

Seriously, let us look to the small business revenue projection methods for inspiration.

The Small Business Revenue Projection Methods—Get Inspired!

The million-dollar question asked by most start-up owners is "How much will I make?" And the million-dollar answer: "If I knew, I would have a million dollars." Revenue projections at best are an accurate forecast and at worst, a good guess. But, if revenues for a financial forecast can be filled in, can the picture of the entire business be painted as well?

The Five Brush Strokes for Revenue Forecasting

1. Gather consumer spending data for the proposed product or service and divide this figure by the total number of competitors.
2. Determine the breakeven point of the new business.

$$BE = FC/1 - (VC/Sales)$$

   Can this be achieved?
3. Survey the target market and ask them, "How much and how often will you spend with me?"
4. Take a friendly noncompetitor out to lunch and ask for pertinent sales data.
5. Conduct a small trial run.

No single stroke by itself paints a complete picture nor do the strokes combined guarantee complete accuracy. The more the merrier, though. These questions, in order, can be answered using public data—the forecasted business expenses—by asking the target market and by opening and operating the business on a small scale. Methods one, three, and four answer how much you should make, method two answers how much you need to make, and method five says "Hey, you are making money now; here's how much you are making."

Together, the answers should paint an overall powerful landscape that answers the question, "How much revenue can I expect to generate?" Remember, this is a forecast; no guarantees here, and certainly crystal balls that predict the future do not exist. If anything, at the center of our painted landscape is a close estimate of the number.

Using our virtual business paintbrush and the five colors mentioned previously, we have painted in from the top, the corners, and the bottom, filling in just about every space except the small space lying at the center. That small space in the center is the million-dollar question, and we've gotten very close to answering it.

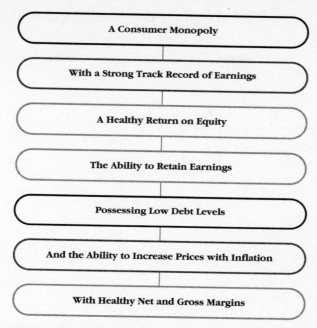

Figure I.1   Building a Small Business Warren Buffett Would Love Flowchart

The same painting methodology used in forecasting revenues can also be applied in building a fundamentally sound, economically strong small business. We are going to get out our brushes, our palette, paint, a giant canvas, and Warren Buffett (don't worry, we have a hand truck), and then we are going to paint our bloody hearts out until all that we have left is a small, tiny spot in the center. Once we have painted a beautiful business landscape, we will hold in our hands the picture of a superior business and revel in the confidence that we have built a small business that Warren Buffett would love. Figure I.1 details the road map we will be following along our journey.

1

Buffett and the Fundamental Business Perspective

He doesn't gamble in the stock market; he doesn't take short-term, technical positions betting on immediate spikes or dips. He is not a buy-and-hold mutual fund investor. Warren Buffett is a long-haul business investor who takes partial, if not whole, positions in companies with favorable underlying economics, good management, and consumer monopolies.

Warren Buffett as Your Small Business Consultant

To draw a quick distinction between a Buffett-style investment and one that is not, ask yourself this question: "In 20 years, is it more likely that consumers will be drinking Coke or using the iPhone?" This question is not designed to play favorites. It is meant to illustrate the guts of the Warren Buffett investment methodology, and if you can understand the reasoning behind the answer, you will be well on your way to building a small business that Warren Buffett would love. In 20 years, is it more likely that consumers will be drinking Coke or using the iPhone?

I choose Coke . . . why? First, four prima facie answers:

1. The company has been building its brand since 1886.[1]
2. A can, bottle, or fountain Coke is always within about a 100-yard reach of every human being on the planet regardless of location.

3. The company had $35 billion in sales last year.[2]
4. Every time I go to the movies, I see a Coke commercial. (Amazingly enough, although polar bears can swim up to 100 miles at a stretch, they are very awkward, lumbering walkers and must kill their prey by resting silently outside of breathing holes in the ice. Even more amazing is the fact that they have enough dexterity in their goofy paws to twist off bottle caps.)

And here are five financial answers that Warren Buffett loves:

1. Outside of a few blips on the radar, the company has had increasing and steady earnings over the past 10 years.
2. The earnings per share have grown at an approximate rate of 13.65 percent over the same period,
3. The return on equity has averaged 32 percent over the past 10 years.
4. The company could pay off its long-term debt in about one year, strictly from earnings.[3]
5. The company can adjust its prices to inflation. In 1950 a bottle of Coke cost a nickel.[4] Today, depending on location, a Coke will cost anywhere from one to two dollars.

The answer to our question and subsequent analysis is not a comment on the viability of Apple or a statement on the quality of the product. Apple is a highly innovative company with outstanding, mind-numbing products. The intention of the answer is to place an emphasis on the predictability of a company. No one can predict the future, but if an attempt must be made (that is, we are building a business that needs to be successful in the future), is it more likely that an accurate prediction can be made based on a rock-solid, consistent track record or on one that is questionable? Not that Apple does not have a strong track record, but guess what, Coke's is stronger. Plus, you are already taking the bet. It's a moot point to say I wouldn't take either one since you are already putting your chips on the table whether by stock purchase, rental property investment, or building a small business that Warren Buffett would love. Since you are joining the party, make sure it is a fun one by taking the surer bet.

Many will argue that past results are not an indicator of future performance, but in the case of Warren Buffett's track record, much of his success can be attributed to a mold of key historic attributes. These attributes, when modeled after in a small business, can lead to great results.

Return on Equity, Return on Investment— the Preview

For any investment decision, whether it be the purchase of a four-plex or the launch of a small business, it is important to calculate the investment's return on investment and return on equity in order to determine if we have a stinker or a winner. (Why would I buy into an investment that churns out a 5 percent return when I can get 10 percent down the road at the local investment farmer's market?) Return on investment is found simply by dividing the business's earnings by the initial investment, whereas return on equity is the earnings divided by the equity in the business found on the balance sheet. These ratios are crucial for investment purposes—crucial, I tell you!

For example: Your business, a hamburger stand, let's call it Sloppy Joe's, consistently generates $10,000 a year in earnings on an initial $50,000 investment for a return on investment of 20 percent. You peer into the feasibility of a second location and determine that Sloppy Joe's Too will generate $1,000 a year in earnings on top of a $25,000 investment for a 4 percent rate of return. A quick Google search reveals that risk-free Treasury bills are paying approximately 4.7 percent,[5] a return slightly higher than the 4 percent that would be churned out by SJ2. The optimal investment decision would be to take the T-bills and not the second location. If you discover another expansion opportunity yielding a return greater than or equal to 20 percent, all things equal, it would be financially prudent to pursue the new opportunity. Honestly, it would be financially prudent to pursue any opportunity that is greater than the return you can get in the next best investment. If you can get 15 percent in the market, then you have to beat 15 percent.

Both rate of return and return on equity can be used to compare investments across asset classes. For example: A dividend-paying stock yielding a 7 percent rate of return for the year is inferior to a rental property returning 15 percent a year, all else equal. A business generating a 4 percent rate of return is inferior to a stock yielding a 6 percent return and, a rental property spewing out a 10 percent return is inferior to a stock that grows in value by 15 percent a year. Got it?

Apples to Apples

A rental duplex cash flow of $5,000 a year on top of a $50,000 investment is providing a 10 percent rate of return (by the way, rate of return and return on investment are the same thing), which is a superior investment compared to a duplex cash flow of $7,000 a year on top of a $100,000 investment for a 7 percent return.

A stock consistently delivering an average 20 percent return on equity, in Warren Buffett's opinion, is in essence delivering a 20 percent rate of return. He claims this return as his (more on this later). A dividend stock paying an annual yield of $.70 with an average price of $10 a share is delivering a 7 percent rate of return. A business with $20,000 in earnings for the year and an initial investment of $100,000 is yielding 20 percent.

In the world of small business and investing, rate of return (return on investment) reigns supreme.

Investing from the Business Perspective

To further illustrate rate of return and how it applies across investments including small business, let us step into the shoes of a rental property investor. A true rental property investor evaluates property based on cash flow and the rate of return. The following table details a cash flow analysis of three sample rental properties, a triplex, fourplex, and duplex respectively. The combination of a down payment, closing costs, and repairs equals the total down payment needed to invest in each of the three properties. These figures are culled from real deals, so don't accuse me of making up some hokey numbers. See Table 1.1.

The cash flow analysis works as follows: The rental income comes in the door, then operational expenses such as vacancy loss, property management fees, accounting, yard work, and repair and maintenance expenses peck away, and what remains is the net earnings or, in a cash budget, the cash flow. In order to calculate the rate of return, annualize the cash flow by multiplying by 12 and dividing by the total property investment, which in this case is $20,750, $26,661,

Table 1.1 Cash Flow Analysis

	1625 Flanigan	1717 O'Shea	1714 O'Brian
Number of Units	3	4	2
Purchase Price	$100,000	$128,304	$97,200
Cash Put into Property			
Down Payment	$20,000	$25,661	$19,440
Closing Costs	$200	$500	$500
Repairs	$550	$500	$200
Total Cash Put into Property	$20,750	$26,661	$20,140
Monthly Cash Flow Analysis			
Gross Rental Income	$1,275	$1,980	$1,350
Less Vacancy Loss 8%	$102	$158	$108
Total Income	$1,173	$1,822	$1,242
Monthly Expenses			
Property Management fee of 10%	$117	$182	$124
Accounting	$10	$15	$5
Insurance	$50	$54	$50
Yard Work	$15	$20	$15
Repairs and Maintenance	$90	$120	$90
Misc.	$10	$15	$10
Reserves	$20	$20	$15
Taxes (Property)	$100	$139	$95
Total Expenses	$412	$565	$404
NOI	$761	$1,257	$838
Loan Payment	$675	$866	$656
Cash Flow	$86	$391	$182
Rate of Return	5%	18%	11%

and $20,140 respectively. This results in a 5 percent, 18 percent, and 11 percent rate of return for each of the properties. All things equal, the property with the 18 percent rate of return is the superior investment.

Warren Buffett applies the same logic to his investment decisions. If he buys a share of stock for $50 and it generates $5 in earnings per share, his initial rate of return is 10 percent. ($5/$50).[6] As the earnings of the company grow, so does the return over time.

This analysis, as used by the rental investor and the Buffett investor, or the hybrid Brental investor, should be the same analysis utilized by the small business owner: A hamburger stand generating $20,000 of yearly earnings on top of a $100,000 investment is generating a 20 percent rate of return. Compared to Treasury bonds, currently yielding approximately 3.5 percent, this is a superior investment.

This, in a nutshell, is investing and building a business via a business perspective.

A Spiel on Capital Gains

Cash flow investors traditionally seek out timely, systemic payments from their assets. For example: A dividend stock investor expects a quarterly dividend payment, a rental property investor seeks a monthly check, a covered call writer often generates income at least once a month. A cash flow investor works for cash flow first and lets capital gains serve as the icing on the cake. If a rental property generates 15 percent a year in cash flow and the property appreciates an additional 4 percent a year, then so be it. The question that cash flow investors traditionally seek to answer is: "Can I pay my monthly bills from cash flow?" If the answer is yes, then the cash flow investor claims financial independence and typically Yahtzee!

The cash flow paradigm is contrasted with that of the capital gains investor. The capital gains investor invests for appreciation of the underlying asset; an asset is purchased for $1 in hope that it will go up to $10, for example. A property capital gains investor will buy a piece of real estate, banking on the appreciation and cashing out at the end, or he will seek to fix and flip the property over the short term. In this way, investors do not necessarily receive monthly cash flow; they can cleave off the capital gains to create a "cash flow," and as long as they do not dip into the principal they have a cash flowing system, although this cleaving will result in a capital gains tax.

Warren Buffett, on the other hand, buys outstanding companies with phenomenal rates of return that continue to reinvest this return and greatly increase the value of the company.

Turning Capital Gains into Cash Flow

Thus, it can be argued that capital gains is essentially "cash flow"; it is just received in larger chunks via systematic withdraws. Mutual fund investors are the best example of this format. A mutual fund investor can theoretically cash out the average gain received on a timely basis, treating it as cash flow. If an individual is banking on an average yearly return of 15 percent, then in theory the investor can cash out 15 percent a year without decreasing the principal. An investor with a $100,000 mutual fund investment, in this example, is counting on $15,000 a year. The problem, of course, lies in the dips. The stock market may average 10 percent over the long run, but some years it may do 20 percent and some years it may do a negative 10 percent.

Let's say in year one your investment makes the projected 15 percent. Everything is fine, you withdraw your $15,000 in cash flow, leaving the $100,000 principal intact. (Tax consequences are ignored for simplicity's sake.) The second year, the investment gains 18 percent. Great! We are living large. Life is good! You can take out up to $18,000 this year and blow it on a boat, if you choose. You play it safe, though, and leave the extra money in place, taking the total principal up to $103,000.

In the third year the stock market tanks and the investment drops by 20 percent to $82,400. Uh-oh . . . danger, danger, Will Robinson . . . batten down the hatches. Now what? The stock is on sale—buy more? But you need $15,000 to live on. If you draw out the $15,000, the principal will be depleted to $67,400 and then, even if the next year returns to normal and generates the average 15 percent return, the investment will only make a little over $10,000. What to do now?

This is where cash comes into play. A capital gains investor should sock away enough cash to weather at least two years of a downturn. In our example, the stashed cash amount is $30,000. Of course, the investment is projected to deliver an average return of 15 percent, so it is not likely that the entire amount will need to be supplemented from cash since the investment will potentially spring back to life at a higher rate. In negative years the cash is used. In positive years the cash is replenished. In this way the capital gains investor becomes a cash flow investor.

Tax consequences cannot be ignored, though. A rental property investor can greatly reduce taxes on the cash flow through depreciation and expense shifting, whereas the mutual fund investor will realize short- or long-term capital gains depending on the invest-ment holding period.

Buffett as a Cash Flow Powerhouse

So, the question is, in order to assist us in building a small business that Warren Buffett would love, which type of investor is Warren Buffett? Is he a cash flow investor or a capital gains investor? The answer is that he is a cash flow investor first, with a catch. A cash flow investor is really a business perspective investor, which is the essence of Warren Buffett's investment soul. He invests in companies with predictable earnings first, just as rental property cash flow investors invest for steady rental checks first. His cash flow is found in the earnings per share that the company generates.[7] The rental property investor's cash flow is found in the rental checks in the mailbox.

The difference between the asset classes is that the stock market is more of a neurotic, schizophrenic beast compared to the real estate market. (The market goes up, the market goes down like a drunken banshee on a daily basis.) But, if the company in question is built upon strong, underlying economics, the equity value of the company will increase and the price will return. This lesson is a piece of the Rosetta Stone necessary to build a small business that Warren Buffett would love. Great companies generate consistent earnings and reinvest them at high returns.

Additionally, Warren Buffett leaves the money within the investment so that it may continue compounding at a high rate of return while avoiding tax consequences. He doesn't need the cash flow. (I think he's going to be okay, you know, for food and whatnot.)

Secondly, he is a capital gains investor because, as any intelligent investor will tell you, capital gains follow cash flow. Buffett argues that retained earnings (read: retained cash flow) add to the company's value and the stock price will eventually rise to realize this. A property investor receives cash flow first (check in the mail) and then can reinvest this cash flow in other rental properties and grow their equity value. In general, a rental property will appreciate in value unless it is in an area of decline. (Or hundreds of banks overextend credit to non-qualified borrowers who subsequently default, but that couldn't happen in a million years, now could it?) Most cash flow investors invest for cash flow first with the principle that capital gains will follow next. Warren Buffett invests for cash flow first (earnings, retained earnings, return on equity), which will add value to the company and lead to business value appreciation.

The Cash Flow Trifecta

A stock that generates strong, consistent, and growing earnings, pays a dividend, and has an option for covered call contracts, is a cash flow powerhouse. And that's all I have to say about that.

How Does This Apply to My Small Business?

Keep in mind three things as we move forward on the tramway of building a small business that Warren Buffett would love:

1. Companies such as Coca-Cola, Kellogg's, and Campbell's have a more predictable nature as a result of strong brand name recognition, consumer appeal, and a healthy, consistent track record of earnings and return on equity.
2. Investing from a business perspective means first and foremost paying attention to earnings and return on equity.
3. Two types of investors exist: the capital gains investor and the cash flow investor. It is important to understand the differences between the two and also where they intersect.

2

The Importance of a Consumer Monopoly or Toll Bridge

When my wife and I popped out our first child (honestly, she did more popping than I did), in addition to the haphazard caches of large plastic cars, ball poppers, and musical tables metastasizing throughout the house like a virus, I noticed another new constant in our lives: Gerber.

Aw, Gerber. The company that has the chubby blue-eyed baby for a logo and that produces just about everything edible for babies.

When Cooper was merely a small gelatinous package slithering around on the floor like Jeff Goldblum at the end of *The Fly*, he ate Gerber Stage Ones, the mushy stuff—the applesauce, the carrots, the sweet potatoes. As he grew into a sturdy "sitter" able to gaze around the room in wonderment, he ate the slightly chunkier stuff, Gerber Stage Twos—the turkey and gravy, chicken and rice, ham and ham gravy, and the Snozzberries! As he evolved into a rampant crawler capable of turning a 360 in two minutes, he moved up to Gerber Graduates—the puffs and crunchies, the even chunkier stuff, the chicken noodle and mixed vegetables and beef. Once he became a sloppy walker, with the gait of a drunkard at last call, he ate the yogurts, the gogurts, the lil' meals, and his favorite of all, the Graduates Ravioli, which comes in an assortment of flavors from chicken and carrot to spinach and cheese.

And yes, folks, this is all made by Gerber. If you have a baby, you will know Gerber.

It occurs to me that Gerber has been around for quite some time and seems to be a staple in every baby's life. I am positive that I ate it as a baby, my parents probably ate it, and my parent's parents probably ate it. A little Google search reveals that Gerber has in fact been around since 1927.[1] Gerber has been stuffing little tikes with ham and ham gravy since before the great depression.

And this, qualitatively, is the essence of a consumer monopoly—a product or service that is a veritable staple in the lives of consumers, whether they wear diapers and stalk parents with the temperament of a zombie, or drive cars and wear adult diapers; most likely, the product has been a staple for quite some time. If you went to the grocery store and this product had suddenly disappeared from all the shelves, you would take note (think Coke, Campbell's, Hershey's, Doritos, Tide, Pepsi, Kellogg's, Gerber). The product is typically something that consumers must have, such as t-shirts and underwear from Fruit of the Loom, chicken noodle soup from Campbell's, insurance from GEICO, or crack from Tebo down the street, and the product or service doesn't necessarily have to be found in the local grocery store (H&R Block, GEICO, or Disney, although I have noticed lots of beady, animated Disney eyes staring out at me from grocery store shelves lately). Just as all roads lead to Rome, all babies go through Gerber.

With a little extra research, I discovered that Gerber is in fact owned by Nestle[2], a conglomerate of consumer monopolies: Purina, Nestlé Crunch, NesCafe, NesQuick, Juicy Juice, and Hot Pockets, to name a few. Walk into any movie theater, look in the candy case, and you will find products all owned by Nestle: Goobers, Raisinets, SnoCaps, Crunch, Butterfinger, and Wonka (Snozzberries). These products are veritable staples in the lives of movie theatergoers and the general public alike, and they can be found in most corner convenience stores.

Briefly Stepping through the Quantitative Mirror

In addition to having an emblazoned brand presence in the minds of consumers, on the quantitative side, a consumer monopoly is cemented in strong earnings and return on equity.

And What It Is Not . . .

The definition of a consumer monopoly can be contrasted and further defined by looking at its antithesis, the commodity-type business, the evil twin! A commodity-type business does not have the consumer brand loyalty of a consumer monopoly. The consumer could care less what name is on the label (think oil, gas, aluminum, steel). In this sense, the businesses within this group are always slugging it out to keep prices low in order to retain and attract new customers. If you are a Coke drinker you are not necessarily going to switch to Dr. Pepper because its two-liter is 25 cents cheaper, but again, if you are sitting at a gas station and the station across the street lowers its gas price by 25 cents, I guarantee you will drive your happy butt across the street for the cheaper gas.

In order to keep prices low these businesses must continually focus on retooling and reengineering for efficiencies. They must typically invest significant amounts in research and development for new products, all within a competitive industry bereft of strong consumer loyalty and leading to tiny squeaks of net margin flatulation. The opportunity to reinvest earnings in new, high yielding opportunities is not available, since most of the margin is eaten away by the retooling and research and development costs. In this regard, return on equity will be much lower compared to the return realized by a consumer monopoly company (low earnings, low return), and thus the three initial staples of consumer brand loyalty, strong earnings, and strong return on equity, are missing within these businesses.

As a small business owner, do not build a commodity-type business. (Do not pass go, do not collect $200 if you do.) The economic current will always be working against you.

What? The Consumer Monopoly and My Small Business

The first question that typically pops to mind in relation to the consumer monopoly type of business and small business is "How the heck can I possibly build the next Coke brand in my lifetime?" And the answer is: You do not have to build the next Coke brand. What needs to happen in order to build a small business that Warren Buffett would love is to build a business that at first is a consumer monopoly in your local market. In other words, you need to build a local brand that is a staple in the lives of local consumers and if it disappeared one day, consumers would take note (Barney's Pool Hall, Lisa's Book Nook, Joe's Volcanic Pizzeria Romp). The question therefore is not "How do I build the next global, billion-dollar sugar water manufacturer?" but "How can my business become a local market consumer monopoly?"

Taking on the Big Boys Is a Big Mistake

The owner of a local pizzeria, Pie in the Sky, has three local competitors: one mom-and-pop and two big boys—Tony's, Domino's, and Papa John's respectively. Let us forget Tony's for a second. If the owner of Pie in the Sky chooses to offer delivery and a reasonably priced pizza of good quality, then all things considered, he is going head to head with Domino's, whose staple business involves reasonably priced pizza of good quality with a delivery option. In my opinion this is a huge mistake, since Domino's has established systems and a nationwide advertising budget of over a million dollars. In head to head competition, Domino's will win.

On the other hand, if the owner of Pie in the Sky builds a Hawaiian themed, luau pizza experience, complete with Elvis and the exploding tomato sauce spewing volcano, which spews every hour on the hour, and no other competitor comes close to replicating this theme, then the business has potential for brand distinction in the minds of consumers. (Again, the local citizenry would take note if the local pizza shop with the exploding volcano all of a sudden closed its doors.) Although it will take more than a tomato sauce spewing volcano and Elvis to build strong brand loyalty and a local market consumer monopoly, this is at least a first step in the right direction and the distinction is clear. Domino's delivers, Pie in the Sky ignites tomato sauce.

Keep this point in mind: It is futile to go head to head with a million-dollar consumer monopoly company unless you own a million-dollar consumer monopoly company. Even then, the question is, as posed by Mary Buffett and David Clark in *Buffettology*, if you had a billion dollars could you successfully take on Domino's or competitively tear each other apart? If the answer is no, then you need to work diligently in creating as much differentiation as possible.

The next step in the analysis is to examine the local mom-and-pop shop competition. Perhaps Tony's pizzeria already has an exploding tomato sauce volcano and consumers associate his pizzeria as the place to go and get covered in tomato sauce while you eat. In this case, it is wise to analyze the competitiveness of Tony's.

Is Tony asleep at the wheel with cockroaches running around the kitchen, or is he a business triathlete who will competively rip your head off and run it up the Rocky stairs in Philadelphia? In my opinion, it would be best to build your branding though differentiation. Why play copycat when you can come up with your own theme . . . say a giant pirate ship in the center of the restaurant instead of an exploding volcano . . . or perhaps just Liza Minnelli sitting on a raft in the middle of a dolphin infested pool singing endless iterations of the *Cabaret* soundtrack?

Differentiation gives the consumer reason to choose pizza joint A over pizza joint B. In the Domino's example, if the pizza between Domino's and Pie in the Sky is the same (flat, round, made of dough, cheese, and tomato paste), after a period of time, theoretically the consumer will be won over by Domino's rapid-fire delivery and competitive pricing. Remember, there are over 7,600 Domino's franchises worldwide,[3] all with buying power leverage and a huge national advertising budget. Without differentiation, Tony's does not stand a chance.

Thus, differentiation and branding are penultimate for the small business in order to build a consumer monopoly and this applies across the small business spectrum, not just to pizzerias. A hamburger stand should not go head to head with McDonald's, just as a tax service provider should not take on H&R Block. Seek to build differentiation in order to become a consumer monopoly in the local market. If that is not possible, then it is imperative to look elsewhere in order to build a small business that Warren Buffett loves.

If You Can't Beat 'Em, Join 'Em—Why a Franchise Makes Sense

As we discuss the consumer monopolies of the world, the Dominoes, McDonald's, and H&R Blocks, it becomes logical to ask, instead of building a consumer monopoly, why not just purchase one? And the reasoning for taking this action is sound: The business will already be an established consumer monopoly and will have a system in place for doing business. Thus, the entrepreneur will not have to reinvent the wheel; although I am not discouraging you from building your own small business. This truly is a book about building a small business that Warren Buffett would love, but just for a second, let us look at this logical option.

Track Records and Subway Cars

Another big advantage of buying a consumer monopoly is that a financial track record already exists. In a pure start-up situation, the financial performance of the business is still basically a guess. In a franchise purchase, a plethora of comparable financials exist. Although the supplied financial franchise track record will not necessarily be tied directly to your local market, comparables for similarly sized markets can be supplied. An individual seeking to franchise a sub-shop in a mid-sized market, for example, should be provided with comparable sub-shop numbers for similar mid-sized markets.

In addition, as a form of insurance, franchises typically do not expand widely until they have a proven business model. Subway, for example, opened 12 working stores before they opened 100. Thus, as a franchisee you have another assurance that the business model works across markets. Just make sure that you are opening a high number store—number 30, 50, or 100—instead of a low number store. In a franchise with a low number of stores, the franchisor is still testing out the business model and it is best not to play the part of a guinea pig.

Make sure as well that the franchise has opened across multiple markets. It is still a business model gamble to open store number 30 in Kentucky if the previous 29 all operate in Wisconsin. (Perhaps Kentuckians won't go for the Cheddar Moose Burger.) There is no proof that the model will work in varying markets and again, in this scenario, the franchise model is still being tested.

Purchasing an Existing Business

If you are seeking to purchase an existing business, whether it is a franchise or not, instead of building a consumer monopoly from scratch, keep in mind the three valuation techniques for putting a price tag on a business.

Comparable Market Analysis

This technique is very similar to the valuation analysis a realtor performs on residential property to determine the selling price. The business owner can obtain recently sold comparable business data from online resources and adjust up or down based on the differences.

Asset Approach

Just as with selling a car and determining the fair market value, with a business you determine the fair market value of the assets and use this to determine the price. As a simple example, let's say you own a lemonade stand along with some mixing spoons, a couple of pitchers, and a box of lemons in inventory. You determine the wooden stand is worth $100 based on the price of the lumber from a local hardware warehouse minus some wear and tear, the spoons are worth $5, the pitchers $10, and the box of lemons cost $25, giving you a selling price of $140. If the buyer is going to assume the debts as well, then simply use the equity in the business as the selling price. For example, if the lemonade stand has $50 in long-term debt, and the purchaser is going to assume this note, then the fair price would be the total asset value of $140 minus the $50 debt for a value of $90.

The Earnings Approach

This method is closest to how Warren Buffett values a stock investment. In this approach, the average earnings from the past three to five years are divided by a capitalization rate, typically the rate of return expected from the investment. Average earnings of $100,000 divided by a cap rate of 20 percent gives you a business value of $500,000. The $500,000 investment provides a 20 percent rate of return. Cap rates are typically bucketed off into four different classes based on the size and type of business.[4]

1. 10 to 15 percent—large-sized businesses, over $10 million in sales.
2. 15 to 20 percent—medium to large-sized businesses with $2 million to $10 million in sales.
3. 20 to 30 percent—small to medium-sized businesses with $500,000 to $2 million in sales.
4. 30 to 50 percent—small-sized retail or service businesses.[5]

With an existing business, ask for the income tax returns; ideally, 10 years' worth.

Keep in mind two things about small business tax returns:

1. Typically, business owners run up as much "other" expenses as possible in order to get a tax break. This is called "expense shifting" and will be detailed in the "other" deductions section.

It includes such things as meals and entertainment, mileage, cell phone, home office, and travel. Add these back in.

2. Most small business owners will tell you they had many cash transactions and underreported income. This is where your personal judgment radar comes into play. Did the business really have twice the amount of income reported, as the owner claims? If you are not comfortable with the numbers or the person, perhaps it is best to walk away.

The Toll Bridge

In the world of Warren Buffett, the toll bridge is similar to the consumer monopoly except the toll bridge is only available option to local consumers, in relation to a product or service, such as a movie theater that is the only one in town. Consumers have no other option if they want to go out to see a movie. They must go through the toll bridge of the single movie theater. As long as competition does not move into town (and customers continue to go out to the movies), the movie theater will continue to benefit from the toll-bridge environment.

It is also not necessary for the toll bridge to have a brand consumer monopoly, although having both is the equivalent of having an economic nuclear weapon. The opposite is inherent—a consumer monopoly builds a brand toll bridge. If you want a Coke, you have to go through Coke.

In the movie theater example, in order to have a solid model, the business should have additional legs to stand on and not rely solely on the fact that it is the only gig in town providing in-demand movies; good customer service; a quality viewing experience; hot, buttery, expensive popcorn; and 3D glasses that make everything appear $3 more expensive. But it is not necessary to dump excessive dollars into bleeding edge technology unless the new project can be justified by its future return.

If a new piece of equipment costs $10,000 and will return $2,000 in additional ticket income per year for a 20 percent rate of return, the owner may elect to move forward on the project if his hurdle rate is, say, 15 percent. Otherwise, the competition is just not present to justify the extra expenses.

Building on this, keep in mind that in analyzing a "go," "no-go" decision for a new project, it is necessary to determine the additional revenues the project will generate.

1. Will the new revenues come about simply via marketing of the new digital projector and the extra attendance this generates?
2. Can an extra $2 be tacked on in order to pay for the new viewing experience?

The second scenario provides a more definitive analysis, since the $2 uptick can easily be multiplied by the average number of yearly tickets sold minus a slight drop-off due to a turn-off factor to arrive at a projected revenue number. The first scenario involves a soft forecast, which can be a good guess at best. How many consumers will truly be enticed by a spanking new digital projector? It might have appeal initially, but soon the new wax coating wears off. I would argue for a synergistic combination of both strategies: Advertise the new projector and bump up the ticket prices by $2. In the analysis, count on a slight increase in traffic due to the marketing of the new projector, which will probably be wiped out by the price increase. Thus, it is prudent to multiply the average number of yearly tickets for the one auditorium by the $2 uptick in price. Additionally, extra expenses to maintain and run the new projector, such as repairs and parts and utilities, must be factored in to arrive at net earnings of the new project.

Of course, technological obsolescence is another factor, in which case the entrepreneur should wait to adopt until absolutely necessary since competition is not a factor.

But I want to build a business that Warren Buffett will love—what the hell are you talking about?

How to Build a Consumer Monopoly

Start by inventorying your local competition; write out the names of competitors, both big boys and small fries. Next to the business names write out the key differentiating aspects of each business. For example, a hamburger stand operator might list McDonald's as a key competitor. The key attributes might be: "largest hamburger stand in the world, reasonably priced, systems-based, enormous buying power, kid-friendly, Hamburgler, Grimace, Officer Big Mac, Mayor McCheese." Now, the big question is, how is your hamburger stand going to differentiate from McDonald's and its $24 billion of revenue from last year?[6] Are you going to offer cheap hamburgers in a systems-based, kid-friendly establishment? I should think not, unless you want to lose your shirt or purchase a McDonald's franchise. McDonald's will win, you will most assuredly die. I will place my money on the golden arches.

Instead, you might offer a premium burger. You might offer a family friendly environment, perhaps in an art-deco restaurant complete with servers dressed as fifties movie characters. The sky is the limit, and it is important. How will you differentiate from the mega burger chains?

Don't forget the small guys either. Even if you are installing a tomato sauce spewing volcano in the center of your establishment and Tony's already has one, you can still probably mooch Tony's customers if Tony does not have all his ducks in a row. But why not create instead of copy? It is much more fun.

Make sure to detail the small guys' differentiating factors and how your business will differentiate in order to build a consumer monopoly that Warren Buffett will love.

Branding

The larger forest that differentiation stands in is branding, and great branding is imperative to building a consumer monopoly. An entire book can be written on the subject of branding, and it has been. Since this is not a treatise on branding, I highly recommend you read and apply *Branding for Dummies,* by Bill Chiaravalle and Barbara Findlay Schenck (John Wiley & Sons, 2006).

Some Branding Pointers

- Brand names are promises—think of Disney, Coke, and McDonald's. What are the branding promises of these companies and how do they deliver on them time and again?[7]
- Brands beat commodities—again, in our Warren Buffett model, consumers have zero loyalty for commodity type businesses such as oil, steel, flour, and milk. A brand inspires love and loyalty.
- Positioning is how you define your product or service in the marketplace and it precedes branding. Leading back to our previous examples of differentiation, you really need to define how your product or service is going to stick out in the minds of consumers.

- At the base of your brand will be the company's mission, vision, values, goals, and leadership. Make sure to have these in place first before building the public facing name, logo, advertising, website, and packaging.
- Once you build your logo, tagline, and overall appearance, continue to be consistent in advertising and marketing. Remember, branding is a long-term effort in order to capture the minds of consumers. McDonald's has not intermittently switched out the golden arches in favor of golden hamburgers, golden french fries, or giant beings with Big Macs for heads, McDonald's has stuck with the arches for more than 40 years, although they gave the boot to the Professor and Captain Crook after only 15 years.

Again, differentiation and branding go hand in hand in building a business that Warren Buffett would love. I highly recommend studying up on the art of branding in order to build a successful consumer monopoly business.

How to Build a Toll Bridge

In your town or region, identify a missing product or service. This might be scathingly obvious (we don't have a movie theater) or it might be fairly subtle (our town of 50,000 has only three tax service providers). Once you have identified a missing need, you should perform some primary marketing research and verify beyond a shadow of a doubt that demand exists for the business. This can be done the old fashioned way with a clipboard and a pencil, or it can be conducted using technological solutions such as Facebook or Survey Monkey. The goal is to verify that consumers will spend often and spend enough to warrant starting the business. It is recommended to build a cash flow projection from this analysis and compute the rate of return.

The Best Combination—A Consumer Monopoly Toll Bridge or a Toll-Nopoly

In a best case, other worldly scenario, your business would be the only establishment in town that serves Coke. (And by Coke, I mean the drink, not the narcotic that makes you feel nuts.) In other words,

Figure 2.1   Building a Small Business Warren Buffett Would Love Flowchart

the business would be a toll bridge and a consumer monopoly rolled into one, the best of both worlds.

It is not necessary for a toll-bridge business to have a consumer monopoly brand to be successful. In our movie theater example, the customers cannot go down the street to the next movie theater because it doesn't exist. Even if they are turned off by the branding, only one gig exists in town. Still, the business with both attributes insures itself against competitive risk through building a distinctive brand, and it insures greater revenues if demand exists. A business that is the only option in town and differentiates itself through some unique form of branding, whether it is through exploding tomato sauce volcanoes, superb customer service, Elvis, Liza Minnelli, or Mayor McCheese's doppelganger, truly sets the stage for superior results and building a business that Warren Buffett would love. Figure 2.1 is the road map for the rest of our journey.

CHAPTER 3

Strong, Consistent, and Growing Earnings

For a business to be successful, it must have strong, consistent and growing earnings over the long term. In part, this chapter provides "Income Statement 101" details and asks you, the small business owner, to review the profit and loss statements over a ten-year period, investigating for strong, consistent, and growing earnings. Start-up business owners should project realistic earnings going forward and look for strong earnings potential. If the earnings do not exist or are not likely to exist, then the question becomes why—why not, by God? If a solution cannot be found, then it is time to reevaluate your situation, kind of like when Lisa Marie Presley realized that her husband climbed "giving" trees and thought he was Peter Pan.

Warren Buffett seeks out businesses with strong, steady 10-year earnings track records.

Through the Eyes of Warren Buffett

In Buffett's world, ownership of a stock means that the earnings belong to you.[1] As a shareholder, you technically own a piece of the underlying business. If you own a 25 percent share in a local hamburger stand, then technically 25 percent of the earnings belong to you. If you own 25 percent of a consumer monopoly company such as Coke, then congratulations, you have more money than almost anybody and need to have me over sometime.

The first sign of a strong business that Warren Buffett loves is found in a rock solid earnings track record that is consistently on the uptick, an indicator that the business can potentially repeat the positive past. We can't predict the future, but when it comes to investments, Warren Buffett has found that the historic earnings track record is a good indicator of the future earnings track record. The lack of a consistent track record is an indicator that predictability is low. (The business has had erratic earnings, going from $.20 a share one year to $1 a share the next, back down to $.60 the following, and so on.)

In the case of a small business, the absence of a strong earnings track record will make it difficult to determine if healthy, growing earnings can be achieved and whether or not the business can eventually be sold for a healthy wad of cash. Keep in mind that the level of expected earnings and the future sales price of the business are two key variables in the world of business. Just as Warren Buffett buys a stock (or an entire business), counting on the eventual price it will reach, you too should start and/or continue to operate a small business based on the eventual sticker price.

Use the earnings picture as the starting point in determining the future value of a business.

Earnings and the Consumer Monopoly

Take a look at Coke's earnings per share for the past 10 years. See Table 3.1. Now look again. What do you see?

Apart from some bumps in the road (in 2002 earnings per share dropped from the previous year's $1.60 to $1.23), we see a strong, steady, and growing track record of earnings. Overall, for this historic 10-year period, the earnings per share for Coke have been growing at a relatively steady 13.7 percent. This picture of steady, consistent, and growing earnings is imperative to the small business income statement if you want to build a business that Warren Buffett would love.

In the realm of small business, the earnings number will not necessarily be on a per-share basis, but you can easily see the earnings picture using historic income statements or tax returns. For example, see Table 3.2.

Ideally, as in the case of Coke's earnings per share, you will see an earnings level that is relatively consistent and growing over time.

Table 3.1   Ten-Year Coke EPS

Year	EPS
1999	$1.30
2000	$1.48
2001	$1.60
2002	$1.23
2003	$1.77
2004	$2.00
2005	$2.04
2006	$2.16
2007	$2.57
2008	$2.49
2009	$2.93

Source: Morningstar.com.

Table 3.2   Small Business Earnings Example

Year	Earnings
1999	$10,000
2000	$10,500
2001	$11,000
2002	$10,250
2003	$11,100
2004	$11,750
2005	$12,000
2006	$11,500
2007	$12,100
2008	$12,500
2009	$12,400

And What We Do Not Want to See . . .

Following is the earnings per share record for a large technology firm. Take a look at this earnings track record in Table 3.3 and note the roller coaster ride.

Back to the theme of predictability: Although past results are not necessarily an indicator of future performance, based on Tables 3.1 and 3.3 for Coke and the technology company, which business are

Table 3.3   Technology Firm Earnings Example

Year	EPS
2001	–$0.36
2002	$0.04
2003	$0.58
2004	$0.00
2005	$0.96
2006	$4.04
2007	$0.40
2008	$0.57
2009	$1.95
2010	$3.85
2011	$7.88

Source: Morningstar.com.

you more comfortable in predicting what the earnings will do next? In other words, which company is more likely to continue producing a record of solid, growing earnings going forward—the one with the solid record of earnings, or the one whose earnings chart mirrors the track layout of Space Mountain? In the world of Warren Buffett, he has found that the company with the steady, growing record of earnings has a much higher degree of predictability.

Again, in 20 years, is it more likely that people will be drinking Coke or using the iPhone, and is it possible that we will have hover boards by then since by all appearances Mr. Spielberg, the 2015 deadline is unlikely. (We only have four years left and I still don't have a self-walking dog collar, a flying car, nor a hydrating microwave oven.)

Why This Is So Important

With predictability comes a greater assurance that the business can repeat the past and has the potential to increase the overall company value. In relation to predictability, there is a cacophony of present valuation formulas that are highly dependent on a continuing earnings picture. Without predictability, these formulas fall apart and we cannot calculate the future value of the business with any sort of reliability. These details will be dissected in later chapters. In addition, a business with earnings can potentially retain the earnings and reinvest them in high yielding projects that will continue to increase the overall company earnings and value.

Where to Start—The Income Statement

The income statement provides the income and expense numbers necessary for determining earnings. See Table 3.4. For churchgoers, you just need to locate the coffee-stained manila folder shoved in the back of your filing cabinet labeled "Taxes" and use the income statements found in the tax returns. For everyone else, use the real numbers found in the second folder labeled with an X.

Let's start there, shall we?

To put the income statement simply: Income minus expenses equals what's left over, which typically boils down to a statement such as "Oh crap honey, you may need to pick up a second job," or "Shhhh, be quiet or the kids will hear that we made money." If you have a positive, black number at the bottom of the income statement, then congratulations, you have net income or earnings. If, on the other hand, you have a red number (or a sort of burgundy, persimmon, or burnt sienna number), then gather up the names, addresses, and phone numbers of three references, head down to

Table 3.4   Sample Income Statement

Sample Income Statement	
Sales (Income)	$25,000
Cost of Sales (COGS)	$9,328
Gross Profit	$15,672
Gross Profit Margin	63%
Payroll/Wages/Salary	$2,153
Rent	$4,650
Depreciation	$3,000
Interest Expense	$1,250
Net Income before Taxes	$4,619
Adjusted Net Income Before Taxes	$4,619
Net Profit Margin	18%
EBITDA	$8,869
Net Income	$3,926

Source: First Research, reproduced with permission.

your local McDonald's, grab a nice warm cup of coffee, ask Skip for an application, sit down, relax, and get to work. See Table 3.4.

Income Statement Forensics

Cost of goods sold includes any costs directly attributed to the product or service: direct labor to make the product, direct materials in the product. For example, let's say that Skip works the grill and fry vat for the day and gets paid $52.50 for his efforts (minimum wage of seven bucks an hour times eight hours minus a 30-minute lunch.) He makes 100 hamburgers, each selling for a buck apiece with about a quarter of food costs in each one. Skip's total wages of $52.50 and the $25 of food costs add up to a cost of goods sold of $77.50. This is not the total COGs for the restaurant for the day. You would have to total all of the direct wages and direct costs . . . I'm just saying.

Subtracting cost of goods sold from sales results in the gross profit, and dividing this number by sales provides the gross profit margin (this is something else we'll later see that Warren Buffett uses his love-radar on). If the business is struggling to produce earnings, gross profit margin is one of the first places to check to see if in fact you are paying too much for the product or perhaps not charging enough, relative to others. If for every dollar in sales, your business is making 50 cents while everyone else is making 60 cents, you are either paying too much for the hamburger buns or not charging enough for the hamburgers.

After gross profit, we drop into the operational expenses of the income statement, expenses such as payroll, rent, interest and, a non-cash item, depreciation. In the context of troubleshooting low earnings, by themselves these numbers are not very helpful. You can analyze for trends across time to see if they are increasing, but context is penultimate in this analysis and common size industry numbers are needed. If net income is lower than the industry average and gross margin is not problematic, then we know that the problem lies somewhere within the operational expenses. Common size industry ratios can be obtained easily from your local banker or Small Business Development Center. See Figure 3.1.

An important factor in building a business that Warren Buffett would love is that you can check the common size statements for healthy, consistent, and growing net margins before or after going

COMMON SIZE STATEMENT

Income Statement Data	June 30, 2009	June 30, 2010	Industry (4913)
Sales (Income)	100%	100%	100%
Net Sales	0%	100%	N/A
Cost of Sales (COGS)	47%	44%	44%
Direct Labor	7%	5%	N/A
Food Costs	39%	38%	N/A
Gross Profit	53%	56%	56%
Depreciation	0%	0%	3%
Amortization	0%	0%	0%
Overhead or S,G,& A Expenses	95%	68%	40%
G & A Payroll Expense	43%	34%	25%
Rent	10%	9%	6%
Advertising	3%	2%	2%
Workers Comp	2%	1%	N/A
Taxes/Licenses	0%	N/A	N/A
Tools/Sm Equipment	2%	0%	N/A
Supplies	9%	3%	N/A
Maintenance	2%	1%	N/A
Car/Travel	1%	1%	N/A
Acct & Legal	1%	1%	N/A
Phone/Internet/Music	1%	0%	N/A
Utilities	5%	4%	N/A
Insurance	2%	0%	N/A
Equipment Rental	0%	0%	N/A
Bank Charges	0%	1%	N/A
Royalty Fees	5%	2%	N/A
Distribution	1%	0%	N/A
Cash Over/Short	0%	0%	N/A
Comps	3%	3%	N/A
Coupons	0%	1%	N/A
Dues Subscriptions	0%	0%	N/A
Laundry/Uniforms	2%	2%	N/A
Credit Card Fees	1%	2%	N/A
Postal	0%	0%	N/A
Gift Cards	N/A	1%	N/A
Outside Services	0%	0%	N/A
Moving Expenses	1%	0%	N/A
Other Operating Income	0%	0%	0%
Other Operating Expenses	0%	0%	10%
Operating Profit	N/A	N/A	4%
Interest Expense	6%	8%	1%
Interest-Loans	0%	8%	N/A
Other Income	0%	0%	0%
Other Expenses	0%	0%	0%
Net Profit Before Taxes	N/A	N/A	3%
Adjusted Net Profit before Taxes	N/A	N/A	3%
EBITDA	N/A	N/A	7%
Taxes Paid	5%	4%	0%
Fixed Payroll Taxes	0%	4%	N/A
Taxes/Sales	0%	N/A	N/A
Extraordinary Gain	0%	0%	0%
Extraordinary Loss	0%	0%	0%
Net Income	0%	33%	N/A
Net Income	N/A	N/A	2%

Figure 3.1 Common Size Income Statement
Source: ProfitCents, reproduced with permission.

into business. This will help in solving the Warren Buffett earnings riddle for your business. If the business is in an industry that produces healthy, growing net margins year after year, it may be possible to repeat these earnings results and build a business Warren Buffett would love. If not, the earnings cards in your industry are stacked against the business, and it is prudent to seek out a more profitable industry.

In the common size statement, the sample data for gross profit are in line with the industry at 56 percent for 2010, including overhead selling, general and administrative expenses, or all direct and indirect expenses linked to the sale of a specific unit. General and administrative expenses (salaries, rent, and utilities) are high at 34 percent compared to 25 percent. The owner of this business would want to dig down into the selling and G&A costs and learn to manage expenses that are out of line with the industry. As you can see, a lot of detail for the industry report is not provided. Thus it might also be prudent to sort the expenses on your income statement from smallest to largest in relation to sales and see if efficiencies can be produced. Month-to-month expense tracking is also highly recommended—if cost of goods sold shoots up to 60 percent one month after averaging 50 percent for the past six, then something is not right, but at least you can manage it now because you caught it through month-over-month monitoring. Also, there is no need to make progress in one month and then backpedal the next.

I Am Purchasing an Existing Business, This as Opposed to I Am Robot

In the case of an existing small business purchase, in keeping with building a business that Warren Buffett would love, it is very important to seek out 10 years' worth of income statements and to examine the track record of earnings. If a solid record of growing earnings is present, is it reliable or is the owner inflating earnings? Can he or she be trusted? "Is our children learning?"[2] Even in the case of a franchise purchase, earnings can be cooked, although it will be harder to hide true performance over a longer period of time such as 10 years. Typically in the case of a sale, book-cooking owners do not have the foresight to start cooking or making corrections 10 years ahead of time.

If the track record of consistent and growing earnings is not present, then the question becomes, "Am I staring at a mismanaged consumer monopoly?" In other words, do you hold in your hands the income statements for a "local Coke brand" that has been in the hands of bad management over the years? If it disappeared off of the face of the earth, even with bad management, would consumers take note and be at a loss as to where they will purchase their non-Coke? In this scenario, serious consideration must be given to the question "Can earnings be improved by increasing revenues, decreasing expenses, or a combination of both over the long term?" If this is not a consumer monopoly business that can be fixed through management, then fundamentally the business has a flat tire and may have permanent, irreparable problems.

In the case of a consumer monopoly, it is difficult even for bad management to permanently damage the sound business model. (New Coke anyone?) Eventually, the bad management will either shape up or ship out and the strong economics of the business will resurface. Warren Buffett likes to invest in businesses that even a bad manager can run because one day, inevitably, "a bad manager will run the business."[3] The strong, consumer-monopoly-like company typically always has the ability to recover.

The question that must be asked, upon the discovery of a poor earnings track record, is: Does the possibility exist that the underlying business is a consumer monopoly? If not, then it is time to move on.

I Am Starting a Small Business

In the case of a business start-up, it is imperative to forecast accurate projections and again, examine for strong earnings. Ideally, as in the case of a franchise, comparable financials will be available and the forecast will be grounded in reality. If it is a pure start-up, then made-from-scratch projections are on the menu.

At the least, five-year financial projections should be developed for the start-up business, and at the most, in keeping with building a business that Warren Buffett would love, 10-year projections should be developed. Keep in mind, the further out the projections are, the less reliable they become.

If earnings do not exist or cannot exist in the projections, then again it is probably time to quietly put the financials down and walk away slowly. If strong, consistent growing earnings exist and you didn't make them up, then Yahtzee!

How to Project

Excellent financial projection software such as South Dakota and Business Plan Pro is available for a nominal cost and should assist you in creating some rock solid projections. Remember, don't kid yourself and make up some kookey number just to please yourself. Your local Small Business Development Center should be able to assist you in developing financial projections for free, although governmental help is always hit or miss depending on whether they show up for work that day. A good set of projections will include at least a five-year balance sheet, income and cash flow statement projections, along with a sources and uses of funds worksheet. A really good set of projections will also include a separate revenue projection, which factors in a start-up curve, seasonality, and revenue from various product or service lines. This is the bomb of financial projections!

Again, the key component to keep in mind at this stage in the game is strong earnings off of the income statement.

Now for the Hard Part

Here is a truth I have discovered in the world of financial projections: It is typically easier to nail down the expenses in a profit and loss projection than the revenues. A realtor can provide rental prices for local commercial properties; the cost of goods sold can be obtained from an industry common size statement; once a location has been settled on, utilities are relatively easy to figure out; insurance quotes can be easily obtained from an insurance agent; payroll can be gleamed from a common size statement. In the restaurant business, typically, 30 percent of sales goes toward food costs, 30 percent to labor, and the rest is used to cover everything else, including net profit; accounting, legal, supplies, maintenance, and so on can be estimated with relative ease.

The real linchpin, the hard part in a start-from-scratch, small business financial projection, is found in the revenue projection. Without any sort of existing track record in place, how the heck does a person project revenues going forward with any type of certainty? Typically, it is wise to try to ground the projections in reality via marketing research and comparable numbers, but even these will provide merely a "modeled" projection. Additionally, revenue projections are never "slightly off" in my experience—they are way off. If the projections are off, the business owner might as well trash the projection, the revenue portion at least, and start over. At this point, however, the entire business was about to be launched based on highly inaccurate projections. Whoops!

I cannot stress enough the power of employing all five revenue projection strategies listed below in painting the small business landscape in order to attempt an accurate revenue projection. The earnings evaluation and the business launch decision depend on it . . . no pressure.

The Five Methods

1. Marketing research
2. A small trial run
3. Reverse engineering the financials
4. Taking a friendly noncompetitor out to lunch
5. Analyzing larger public companies

Marketing Research

Yes, there is such a thing as primary and secondary marketing research, just as Virginia was lied to and told there was a Santa Claus, but what really helps the small business owner the most is primary marketing research—or getting out there, pressing the flesh, and asking the customers what they want. Using surveys and focus groups, find out how much and how often the consumer will spend money on your product or service. If the answer is nothing or never or "get away from me," then perhaps it is time to come up with a new business concept.

Using the data collected, if 10 percent of the target market surveyed respond that they will in fact spend on average $10 a week on your product or service, then through extrapolation, it can be determined, based on the number of folks in the target market, how many consumers will purchase from you. This may mean that out of 50,000 consumers in the local market, 20,000 may be within the defined target market (buyers of pizza, let's say), and out of this target market 10 percent or 2,000 will spend $10 a week on your product for a total of $20,000 a week or just over a million bucks a year. That is a lot of pizza!

The "Splitting the Pie" Method of Marketing Research

Also, you can typically obtain local market consumer spending data from local resources such as the Chamber of Commerce or Small Business Development Center. This data will tell you, for example, how much local consumers are spending on various industrial sectors such as durable goods, retail clothing, and Madonna albums. You can then take this dollar amount and divide it by the number of competitors in the area (yours included as well) and determine an evenly split revenue pie number. For example, in consulting with the owner of a small outdoor retail supply business, I discovered from spending data that consumers in the area were spending approximately $500,000 a year on outdoor supplies. With five outdoor retail supply businesses in the area, an even split in the demand will result in $100,000 of potential revenues for the new business.

Of course, this is very unrealistic. The pie will not be split evenly. Some businesses are going to be more competitive than others; some are going to have cardboard boxes for mattresses in the back office. Therefore, adjustments up and down should be made based on some sort of qualitative/quantitative guess as to the competitiveness of each competitor. Investigate the establishments, ask customers, look for cardboard box mattresses in the back.

A Small Trial Run or, Just Open the Doors and See What Happens—Hello World!

Since the most reliable revenue indicator is a live track record, why not just start the business and see what happens? Instead of throwing an entire life savings and kitchen sink into the deal by starting big, start small and see how the business performs. This is still a test, after all, to see if steady earnings can be achieved in order to build a small business that Warren Buffett would love. Start in a small rental space, at a local flea market perhaps, manufacture a small batch of prototypes and see if they sell. Anything to mitigate the risk of a full, lunatic launch in order to determine whether earnings-generating demand exists out there.

Reverse Engineer the Financials

Instead of asking how much can I make, ask how much do I need to make? Find the break-even point for certain sales levels and ask, "Is this obtainable?"

The break-even formula:[4]

$$BE = FC/1 - (VC/Sales)$$

$$FC = \text{fixed costs}$$

$$VC = \text{variable costs}$$

To find the numbers that go into this, simply take your first year projected income statement, identify all of the costs that are variable and all that are fixed—variable costs such as cost of goods sold will fluctuate with sales while fixed costs such as rent will remain relatively static. Total them up and plug them into the formula. If you must sell $100,000 worth of pizzas in order to break even, is this reasonable? That sounds like a lot of pizza to me.

Take a Friendly Noncompetitor Out to Lunch

No one is simply going to dish up sales information just because you ask in a friendly "Bob's your Uncle" manner, but if you ask the right person, perhaps a business owner whose business is located in a separate noncompeting, similar size market, and approach him in a principle-centered, mentor/apprentice manner, the owner might be willing to share some information with you. He might not perhaps provide spot-on, detailed data (as in, here's my tax return and here's how much cash I'm not reporting), but perhaps will be willing to provide a reasonable demand picture that will assist in fitting another piece into the puzzle.

Analyzing Larger Public Companies

In developing the revenue projection for the outdoor retail supply store, I used public financial data to develop a sales projection. Using Internet databases, large public retail chain sales data was obtained and "normalized" for the local market, in order to reach a revenue projection for the fishing and camping store. In other words, based on the size of the client's market compared to the average size of the retail giant's typical market, sales numbers were adjusted down. The lack of a million-dollar advertising budget as opposed to the mega-chains' endless gobs of money, and the lack of 50 years worth of brand-building as opposed to Coke commercials in every movie theater, were factored in as well.

Logical: yes. Accurate? I never felt comfortable with this method since too many unknown variables exist, and it is very difficult to compare a business start-up to a large, well-established, national chain. So no, not very accurate at all, I must say. Still, this method can assist in painting the overall demand picture.

Bottom Line

In the case of a business start-up, the million-dollar question always is: "How much can I expect to make?" And again, if you can answer this question, then in theory you should have a million bucks— either that, or at the least a really good psychic hotline business. In the case of building a business that Warren Buffett would love, we want to determine whether the business can produce a strong 10-year track record of earnings and then from there, waterfall into the other Buffett parameters such as return on equity, retained earnings, and low debt levels. Remember, Buffett does not invest in businesses without, at minimum, a 10-year track record of strong earnings.[5] The entrepreneur in a pure business start-up situation is investing in a business that does not have a track record, kind of like investing with your pants dropped around your ankles.

Application for Small Businesses

For existing owners, it is imperative to review the income statement on a regular basis. Is the business producing steady, growing earnings? If not, why not? Can it be fixed? In order to replicate the brush strokes of a consumer monopoly, the business must have consistent and growing earnings. The question is: Do the earnings dip year to year? If so, why? Are opportunities around to grow earnings by increasing income and decreasing expenses? Remember, earnings cull from a good old income statement:

$$Income - Expenses = Earnings$$

As Ben Franklin said, "the accumulation of wealth is a matter of augmenting means and diminishing wants." (In addition to "A countryman between two lawyers is like a fish between two cats.") The same goes for earnings. Can you expand profitably or adopt a marketing strategy to increase income? Can operational expenses be trimmed? Can the product be bought cheaper while maintaining a standard of quality? I highly recommend obtaining common size industry financials from your local bank or Small Business Development Center. These will allow you to compare your expenses using common size ratios.

Understand also that as sales dip, expenses must be monitored and cut in order to maintain a steady level of earnings year after year. Some expenses such as the light bill and rent will remain static. Others such as labor and supplies can be managed. Maintain efficiencies and expand into good investments that reap large rates of return. Review the financial statements on a regular basis. Monitor and manage the earnings.

The Initial Rate of Return on a Stock—The Initial Rate of Return on a Business

If you buy a stock for $100 and it has net per share earnings of $10, your initial rate of return is 10 percent. The same calculation holds true for a small business: If you purchase a small business for $100,000 and it has average yearly earnings of $10,000, your initial rate of return is 10 percent.

Now, will these rates of return continue? It all comes back to the predictability of earnings, and Warren Buffett has found that the businesses with the highest levels of predictability are the ones with a consistent earnings track record. See Table 3.5.

Warren Buffett invests in companies with the ability to grow their earnings. Thus, in the world of Warren Buffett, the initial rate of return is growing at the same rate as the company's earnings growth. This earnings growth rate can be found by applying the time value of money, future value formula, using a historic earnings number as a present value, a current earnings number for a future value, the number of years in between, and by solving for the interest rate.

For example, in 2000 and 2010 McDonald's had earnings per share of $1.46 and $4.58, respectively.[6] The inputs in our handy dandy BAII Plus financial calculator are as follows:

$$PV = \$1.46$$

$$FV = \$4.58$$

$$N = 10$$

$$CPT \ I/Y = 12.11$$

Thus, on average, the 10-year historic earnings for McDonald's have grown at a rate of 12.11 percent. What this means is that with McDonald's at a current price of $81.14 and recent earnings per share of $4.58, if the stock were purchased today, the initial rate of return would be 6 percent ($4.58/$81.14) and this rate of return, in theory, will be growing at 12.11 percent a year. So, by the end of year one, the earnings should grow to $4.85. At the end of year two, $5.15; year three, $5.45, and so on. By the end of year three, the rate of return on the initial investment would be 7 percent ($5.45/$81.14). Not too shabby.

Discounting

A dollar today is not worth as much tomorrow if you do nothing with it, like bury it in the backyard or spend it on booze. In the world of Warren Buffett, the value of a business can be found by taking its yearly earnings, calculating the future value, and then discounting back to present value. These calculations can be made very easily using a BAII Plus financial calculator.

Table 3.5   Earnings Predictability

This . . .		Not This . . .	
Year	EPS	Year	EPS
1999	$1.30	2001	($0.36)
2000	$1.48	2002	$0.04
2001	$1.60	2003	$0.58
2002	$1.23	2004	$0.00
2003	$1.77	2005	$0.96
2004	$2.00	2006	$4.04
2005	$2.04	2007	$0.40
2006	$2.16	2008	$0.57
2007	$2.57	2009	$1.95
2008	$2.49	2010	$3.85
2009	$2.93	2011	$7.88

If you have a hamburger stand generating $1,000 a year in earnings, in 10 years you will have $10,000. But if you also invest those earnings along the way, let's say at 9 percent invested monthly, you will have $16,126.

Here are the inputs for your financial calculator:

$$P/Y = 12$$

$$N = 120$$

$$I/Y = 9$$

$$PMT = -\$83.33 \text{ (monthly earnings, \$1,000 / 12)}$$

$$CPT\ FV = \$16,126$$

Now, keep in mind that this is the future value, and our task is to find the price we would be willing to pay today in order to receive this future value of $16,126. (Remember how Wimpy from Popeye used to say "I'll gladly pay you Tuesday for a hamburger today"?[7] Well, he was one smart bastard because if someone ever took the deal, Wimpy could invest the dollar, pay off the hamburger, and with the interest gained, come out ahead.)

To determine what we would be willing to pay, if we determine that we can invest at a 9 percent rate, we simply discount the future value back to the present value using the 9 percent discount rate. This is the price we should pay for the right to receive the business's future cash flows.

Inputs:

$$P/Y = 1$$

$$N = 10$$

$$I/Y = 9$$

$$FV = -\$16,126$$

$$CPT\ PV = \$6,812$$

Thus, for a hamburger stand business generating $1,000 a year in earnings with a reinvestment rate of 9 percent, we should be willing to pay $6,812 for the business today. If you want a higher rate of return, say 15 percent, then simply use 15 percent to find the present value of the future cash flows.

$$\textbf{P/Y} = 1$$

$$\textbf{N} = 10$$

$$\textbf{I/Y} = 15$$

$$\textbf{FV} = -\$16,126$$

$$\textbf{CPT PV} = \$3,986$$

If we wish to earn a 15 percent rate of return on our investment, then we need pay no more than $3,986 for the business. And if you want a really good deal, then gladly pay them Tuesday for the business today.

Six Degrees of Hypersensitive Separation

Although 9 percent and 15 percent are separated by only six points, remember how sensitive the time value of money is to rate changes. Table 3.6 reflects an investment of $10,000.

Over a 60-year period, the 6-point difference leads to a $42 million difference! Wowzers! Emphasizing the rate of return in a business investment decision, whether it be the purchase of an entire business or a business expansion project, is one of the first steps in building a small business that Warren Buffett would love.

Table 3.6 $10,000 Invested

# of Years	at 9 %	at 15 %
5	$15,386	$20,114
10	$23,674	$40,456
15	$36,425	$81,371
20	$56,044	$163,665
25	$86,231	$329,190
30	$132,677	$662,118
35	$204,140	$1,331,755
40	$314,094	$2,678,635
45	$483,273	$5,387,693
50	$743,575	$10,836,574
60	$1,760,313	$43,839,987

So What? How Does This Apply to My Small Business?

Once you have found the business value by first projecting the future value and then discounting it back to a present value based on a desired rate of return, you next apply the earnings growth rate as found earlier in the McDonald's example. Simply take the business earnings from 10 years ago and the current earnings level (if this is a case of a start-up with no track record then use the projections), use 10 for the number of years, and compute the rate of return. For example, if a business had $700 a year in earnings 10 years ago and current earnings of $1,000 a year, the financial calculator inputs will be:

$$PV = -\$700$$

$$FV = \$1,000$$

$$N = 10$$

$$CPT\ I/Y = 3.63$$

Building from our previous example, this means that if you buy the hamburger stand at $3,986 for a 15 percent rate of return, the earnings will continue to grow at a rate of 3.63 percent a year.

Take Away

- Warren Buffett seeks out businesses with strong, 10-year earnings track records, which are an indicator of strength and predictability.
- This track record is found in the income statement.
- An existing business has a track record in place.
- A solid franchise has a track record in place.
- A start-from-scratch, small business owner must develop and rely on projections to describe the earnings.
- Common size statements can be used to determine if strong earnings are present at an industry level and can assist in troubleshooting earnings.
- You can use the earnings of the business to project a future business value and discount to the present value to determine a reasonable purchase price.

- McDonald's is notorious for dumping useful and relevant mascots such as the Professor, who spent his time inventing and researching new food patents, in favor of mascots whose usefulness is less apparent. Birdie the Early Bird for example is a "clumsy" bird who can't fly, and the McNuggett Buddies are, and I quote "a bunch of chicken nuggets in regular size."[8] Figure 3.2 indicates our location on the road map.

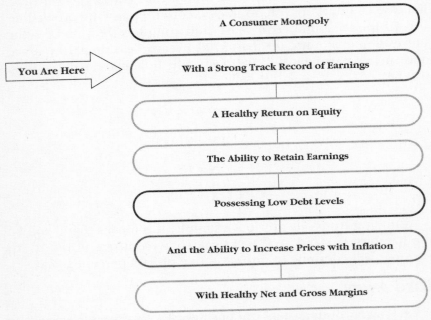

Figure 3.2   Building a Small Business Warren Buffett Would Love Flowchart

CHAPTER 4

Emphasizing a High Return on Equity

A business first and foremost in the realm of Warren Buffett is an investment; it is not merely a job or a means to an income, or a place to hang out as seen through the typical eyes of a small business owner. Although personal income is certainly a priority in small business, it should always be subordinated to the business as an investment in order to build a small business that Warren Buffett would love. In traversing the road from small business owner with an emphasis on income to small business owner with an emphasis on investment, it is imperative to calculate the business's return on equity on a regular basis. Warren Buffett considers the return on equity to be his rate of return in the stocks of the companies he invests in.[1] A small business owner with a focus on return on equity can evaluate the business based on return, determine if it is generating a strong or mediocre return, make a forward-moving investment decision, and sound good in a bar, all in one fell swoop.

Painting the Picture of Return on Equity

Simply put, return on equity is a measure of how hard the equity in a business is working.

$$ROE = Net\ Income/Shareholder's\ Equity$$

Net income can be found on the income statement and equity can be found on the balance sheet. In a small business with one owner, all of the equity technically belongs to the single owner or the single shareholder, although technically, shares may not exist depending on the entity type. All things equal, a business investment with a 20 percent return on equity is superior to a business investment with a 10 percent return on equity.

Why So Important?

As you can see from our ROE formula, a business with a strong return on equity is delivering a healthy amount of income using the least amount of equity possible. (The numerator is big, the denominator is small, you put the lime in the coconut.) Back to our comparison mantra, we don't necessarily want to throw $100,000 worth of equity into a business generating a 10 percent return on equity, or $10,000 a year, when we can invest it in another available option that is firing at 20 percent a year and will deliver $20,000 a year in income. More is better, right, when it comes to income and business.

For an existing business, a low return on equity is an indicator of a problem. If after obtaining your handy dandy industry comparison report you find that your business should be chopping away at a 15 percent return on equity and it is only delivering 7 percent, I would argue that the competition in town is probably eating your lunch (McNuggets included), and sooner or later they will be eating your dessert as well (Snozzberries!). The competition is utilizing their equity more efficiently, leaving them more income at the end of the year to potentially reinvest and grab more market share. Better start tweaking your return on equity or grabbing those McDonald's references.

And Now Some Examples

Table 4.1 displays three 10-year track records of three consumer monopoly companies that Warren Buffett was at one time or currently in love with: McDonald's, Coke, and Wal-Mart. Above all else, this picture should give you a crystal clear expectation of what to look for in order to build a business that Warren Buffett would love. Remember, return on equity is found by dividing the net income, from the income statement, by the equity found on the balance sheet.

Table 4.1   Ten-Year Return on Equity for Three Consumer Monopolies

	MCD	KO	WMT
2001	17.51%	38.38%	20.08%
2002	9.04%	26.33%	21.60%
2003	13.22%	33.58%	21.83%
2004	17.40%	32.29%	22.08%
2005	17.73%	30.18%	21.90%
2006	23.16%	30.53%	19.67%
2007	15.58%	30.94%	20.18%
2008	30.01%	27.51%	20.63%
2009	33.20%	30.15%	21.08%
2010	34.51%	42.32%	23.53%
Average	21.14%	32.22%	21.26%

Source: ProfitCents, reproducd with permission.

McDonald's: The name alone brings to mind those golden, crispy fries, inexpensive hamburgers, Grimace, Officer Big Mac, Mayor McCheese, the useless McNugget mascots.

Look at that golden, crispy return on equity over the years. Despite a very anemic 2002 at 9 percent, we see a steady, strong march through the mid to upper teens and into the lower 30 percent range in the late 2000s, resulting in a hearty, 10-year average return on equity of 21 percent. Beat that Colonel Sanders! (Author's note: The squinty eyed, bolo-tie wearing, senior commissioned officer connoisseur of fried poultry has in fact annihilated this number . . . over the past five years, as part of the Yum brands portfolio, according to Morningstar.com, KFC and its Yum counterparts have averaged a 131 percent return on equity. That's a lot of chicken!) McDonald's exemplifies a business with steady, strong, and growing return on equity, one that so far, Warren Buffett would love.

Coke: In my opinion, Coke nowadays is synonymous with the American flag (and not so much feelings of well-being, euphoria, and enhanced motor skills) . . . that's what over 100 years of brand-building will do for you. I am willing to bet that most Americans (and most global inhabitants) are always a stone's throw away from an ice cold Coke. Coke has been a favorite of Warren Buffett's for years. He first purchased $1 billion worth of Coke stock in 1988[2] and infamously drinks Cherry Coke hand over fist. We can see from

Table 4.1 that Coke consistently hovers around a 30 percent ROE and has averaged 32 percent. Not too shabby . . . it sure beats the Hamburgler. (Of course, it still can't hold a candle to the beady-eyed Colonel and his extra crispy drumsticks.)

Wal-Mart: Whether you love 'em or hate 'em, this bargain barn has generated a healthy 21 percent return on equity over the past 10 years. This company over the years has delivered a consistent 20 percent return on equity with the reliability of Old Faithful. Time and again, Wal-Mart has proven its ability to generate a healthy return on equity and sell tons of plastic whiskbrooms.

Return on Equity Industry Averages

The following ROE industry tables, although not all inclusive, are fairly wide-spanning and should provide you with a bull's-eye for a return on equity target. Not doing so hot compared to the industry? Time to roll up the sleeves and stick your hands in. Don't see your industry in Table 4.2? Hit up your local banker or Small Business Development Center for some RMA reports.

Another Reason Return on Equity Is So Doggone Important

One magical word: compounding.

The reason why return on equity is so important to the small business owner turned small business investment owner is the magical phenomenon of compounding. Table 4.3 illustrates the effects of compounding returns by comparing two initial investments of $10,000, the first of which is compounding at 10 percent and the second is compounding at 20 percent over 5-, 10-, and 15-year periods. What you find is a magical, metastasizing snowball of wealth, each layer of snowflake dollars compounding on top of the last and forming an avalanche of wealth.

Investment One, growing at 10 percent per year, inflates to $16,105, $25,937, and $41,772 over 5, 10, and 15 years respectively. Investment Two grows to $24,883, $61,917, and $154,070 over the same time period. Over the same 15-year time period, at a rate of return of 20 percent, the second investment grows to a value that is $112,298 greater than investment One growing at 10 percent! That is a huge difference in snowflakes and magic.

Table 4.2 Five-Year Average ROE by Industry

Industry	Average 5-Year ROE	Industry	Average 5-Year ROE	Industry	Average 5-Year ROE
Accident and Health Insurance	9.1	Business Services	17.9	Education and Training Services	25.9
Advertising Agencies	16.3	Business Software and Services	13.4	Electric Utilities	28.8
Aerospace/Defense—Major Diversified	23.9	Catalog and Mail Order Houses	15.6	Electronic Equipment	13.8
Aerospace/Defense—Products and Services	15.2	Cement	13.1	Electronics Stores	19.5
Aluminum	8.9	Cleaning Products	13.7	Electronics Wholesale	10.9
Apparel Stores	27.5	Computer Based Systems	14.9	Entertainment—Diversified	20.6
Appliances	17.4	Computer Peripherals	10.5	Farm and Construction Machinery	16.7
Application Software	18.5	Confectioners	23.6	Farm Products	12.3
Asset Management	14.1	Conglomerates	54.5	Food Wholesale	19.2
Auto Dealerships	9	Consumer Services	50.4	Gaming Activities	20.8
Auto Parts Stores	68.5	Credit Services	23.6	Gas Utilities	20.8
Basic Materials Wholesale	15	Dairy Products	27.8	Home Improvement Stores	16.9
Beverages—Brewers	14.2	Department Stores	12.4	Hospitals	15.5
Beverages—Soft Drinks	19.9	Discount, Variety Stores	11.6	Housewares and Accessories	11.3
Beverages—Wineries and Distillers	17.3	Diversified Communication Services	15.1	Independent Oil and Gas	25
Broadcasting—Radio	8.7	Diversified Utilities	10.6	Industrial Electrical Equipment	14.9
Broadcasting—TV	16.8	Drug Related Products	24.3	Industrial Equipment and Components	89.8
Business Equipment	150.5	Drug Stores	16.3		

(Continued)

Table 4.2 (Continued)

Industry	Average 5-Year ROE	Industry	Average 5-Year ROE	Industry	Average 5-Year ROE
Industrial Equipment Wholesale	17.5	Machine Tools and Accessories	9.7	Office Supplies	11
Industrial Metals and Minerals	63.8	Management Services	25.5	Oil and Gas Drilling and Exploration	21.8
Information and Delivery Services	62.5	Manufactured Housing	18.6	Oil and Gas Equipment and Services	18.3
Information Technology Services	14.6	Marketing Services	30.2	Packaging and Containers	290.3
Insurance Brokers	11.7	Meat Products	12	Paper and Paper Products	18.7
Internet Information Providers	428	Medical Appliances and Equipment	67.8	Personal Computers	41.8
Internet Service Providers	51.9	Medical Equipment Wholesale	11	Personal Products	27.7
Internet Software and Services	20.7	Medical Practitioners	10.6	Personal Services	77.1
Investment Brokerage—National	13.6	Metals Fabrication	19.4	Photographic Equipment and Supplies	9.1
Investment Brokerage—Regional	12.8	Mortgage Investment	10.4	Pollution and Treatment Controls	8.4
Jewelry Stores	8.6	Movie Production, Theaters	79.8	Printed Circuit Boards	13.2
Life Insurance	8	Multimedia and Graphics Software	30.5	Recreational Vehicles	22
Lodging	25.8	Music and Video Stores	14.5	REIT—Diversified	10.8
Long-Term Care Facilities	32.9	Networking and Communication Devices	14.8	REIT—Healthcare Facilities	10.1
Lumber, Wood Production	26.4	Nonmetallic Mineral Mining	22	REIT—Hotel/Motel	2.8
				REIT—Industrial	5.6
				REIT—Office	7

REIT—Residential	8.5	Small Tools and Accessories	13.1	Textile—Apparel Clothing	24.5
REIT—Retail	16.4	Specialized Health Services	23	Textile—Apparel Footwear and Accessories	16.8
Rental and Leasing Services	11.8	Specialty Chemicals	26	Textile Manufacturing	7.5
Research Services	16.6	Specialty Eateries	16.1	Tobacco Products, Other	11.8
Residential Construction	12.4	Specialty Retail, Other	533.1	Toy and Hobby Stores	9
Resorts and Casinos	10.6	Sporting Activities	851.7	Toys and Games	10.8
Restaurants	26.6	Sporting Goods	10.9	Trucking	15.3
Rubber and Plastics	17.9	Sporting Goods Stores	15.4	Trucks and Other Vehicles	13.4
Savings and Loans	6	Staffing and Outsourcing Services	9.3	Waste Management	35.8
Security and Protection Services	11.8	Surety and Title Insurance	6.5	Water Utilities	8.5
Security Software and Services	12.7	Technical and System Software	12.4	Wholesale, Other	10
Shipping	26.2	Technical Services	11.2	Wireless Communications	67.9

Source: iclub.com, reproduced with permission.

Table 4.3   Compounding Magic

	Investment One at 10 Percent	Investment Two at 20 Percent
5 years	$16,105	$24,883
10 years	$25,937	$61,917
15 years	$41,772	$154,070

Table 4.4   Ultimate Compounding Magic

	Investment One at 10 percent	Investment Two at 20 percent
30 years	$174,494	$2,373,763
40 years	$452,593	$14,697,716

By years 30 and 40 the differences are staggeringly dramatic and ridiculous: Investment Two will have grown to $2,373,763 and $14,697,716 respectively, versus investment One, which will have grown to $174,494 and $452,593, creating spectacular, chasm differences of just over 2 million and 14 million respectively. Perhaps "magic" is not an accurate descriptor of the multi-cylindered compounding effect. Perhaps "nuclear reactor" or "galaxial force" or "roller skate with a rocket attached" hits closer to home. See Table 4.4.

To Rent or Not to Rent, That Is the Question

Rental property financials always provide a good illustration of return on equity. Table 4.5 is a sample rental property income statement. Again, folks, no hoax here, this is the real deal.

You can see in this example that the rental property generates earnings of $3,264. With an initial investment of $20,750, this earnings level results in a return on investment of 26 percent ($9,480/$37,000), which in this example is the initial return on equity. As time goes by and loan payments are made, the equity in the rental will increase, so by the end of the first year, return on investment and return on equity will be two different beasts altogether.

Some Definitions

You didn't think I was going to leave you hanging on those investment terms, did you?

Return on Equity = Earnings/Equity

Return on Investment = Earnings/Initial Investment

Rate of Return—Same as return on investment. Some people just like to throw this term around because it helps them to sound good at a bar.

Cash Flow—Technically, this is the change in cash on the cash flow statement after all sources and uses of cash have been accounted for. The cash flow statement includes all sources and uses of cash from operations, financing, and investment activities. The net change in cash equates to how much cash the business earned in

Table 4.5 Rental Property Income Statement: The Sample

	1625 O'Flanigan
Number of Units	3
Purchase Price	$100,000
Cash Put into Property	
Down Payment	$20,000
Closing Costs	$200
Repairs	$550
Total Cash Put into Property	$20,750
Yearly CF Analysis	
Yearly Gross Rental Income	$18,000
Minus Vacancy Loss of 8 percent	$1,440
Total Income	$16,560
Yearly Expenses	
Property Management Fee of 10 percent	$1,656
Accounting	$120
Insurance (Hazard)	$600
Yard Work	$180
Repairs and Maintenance	$1,080
Misc.	$120
Reserves	$240
Taxes (Property)	$1,200
Total Expenses	$5,196
NOI	$11,364
Loan Pmt	$8,100
Earnings	$3,264
Rate of Return	16%

the period. In the world of selling purple books to the masses by the bucketful, Robert Kiyosaki in *Rich Dad, Poor Dad* describes cash flow as the amount of money an asset puts in your pocket each month.[3]

Okay, Nice Definitions—So What? How Does This Apply to My Small Business and Building a Business That Warren Buffett Would Love?

Okay, hold your horses, I am getting to the point. Remember, Warren Buffett looks for businesses with high return on equity compared to other businesses (both within an industry and across), plus consistency. The business needs to prove that it can continue to perform at this return level time and again and that it is not merely some freak putting on a fading performance. The return on equity needs to be strong and steady over time.

It is important to monitor and manage the return on equity in a small business in order to build a beast that Warren Buffett would love, but before we tackle a specific application, let us break apart ROE and look at the mechanics of the ratio.

Breaking Up Is Hard to Do

The following Tables 4.6 and 4.7 illustrate the effects of varying levels of equity and earnings on the ROE equation. The first plays around with the amount of equity in the business. The second illustrates varying levels of earnings.

You can see that in Table 4.6, as equity decreases and earnings stay the same at $9,480, return on equity goes up. In Table 4.7, as earnings increase and equity stays the same at $37,000, return on equity again goes up. This is really just simple divisional math at work. The larger the bottom part (the denominator) the smaller the result. The larger the top part (the numerator) the larger the result. In our case, the numerator is earnings and the denominator is equity.

Table 4.6   Static Earnings, Dynamic Equity

Equity	Earnings	ROE
$50,000	$9,480	19%
$37,000	$9,480	26%
$10,000	$9,480	95%

Table 4.7   Static Equity, Dynamic Earnings

Equity	Earnings	ROE
$37,000	$5,000	14%
$37,000	$9,480	26%
$37,000	$15,000	41%

So it goes without saying, in order to have a healthy return on equity, use the smallest amount of equity possible in order to generate the largest amount of earnings possible.

A simple recipe, right?

Okay, Now for the Applicable Small Business Part—See, I Told You I was Getting to the Point

Let us see how return on equity applies to the world of business.

Return on Equity from a Business Perspective

In the following sample income statement (Table 4.8) for Joe's Hamburger Stand, we find an initial rate of return of 17 percent. Joe initially put $20,000 into the hamburger stand and generated $4,350 in net income the first year. Not too shabby, Joe!

This initial rate of return is the same as the initial return on equity. Joe buys the assets with his investment capital, and assets minus liabilities is equal to equity. Thus, at the start of the deal, equity and investment are the same. Once the equity in the business changes from the initial investment, the rate of return will differ from the return on equity, and it will be necessary to pull the equity off the balance sheet in order to calculate the return on equity.

For example, let's say that by the end of year two Joe generates $4,700 in hamburger stand earnings. Let's also assume that Joe has paid down his long-term debt from $100,000 to $80,000; thus, for simplicity's sake, the equity has gone up from $20,000 to $40,000. (See Tables 4.9 and 4.10.)

With consistent earnings of $4,700 Joe's return on equity has actually gone down to 11.75 percent! ($4,700/$40,000). Since Joe is now employing more equity, the bottom part of our equation, the denominator, has gotten larger, thus reducing the result. Joe had

Table 4.8   Joe's Hamburger Stand Income Statement

Joe's Hamburger Stand	
Initial Investment	$20,000
Revenues	$80,000
COGs	$24,000
Gross Income	$56,000
Expenses	
Payroll	$20,000
Payroll Taxes	$2,550
Supplies	$1,500
Maintenance	$2,700
Marketing/Advertising	$1,400
Car/Travel	$300
Accounting and Legal	$500
Rent	$9,600
Phone	$900
Utilities	$1,500
Insurance	$1,200
Interest	$7,000
Depreciation	$2,500
Total Expenses	$51,650
Net Income	$4,350
Initial Rate of Return	22%

Table 4.9   Joe's Balance Sheet Beginning of Year

This . . .	
Assets	
Current Assets	$30,000
Fixed Assets	$100,000
Total Assets	$130,000
Liabilities	
Current Liabilities	$10,000
Long-Term Liabilities	$100,000
Total Liabilities	$110,000
Equity	$20,000

**Table 4.10   Joe's Balance Sheet
End of Year**

Becomes This	
Assets	
Current Assets	$30,000
Fixed Assets	$100,000
Total Assets	$130,000
Liabilities	
Current Liabilities	$10,000
Long-Term Liabilities	$80,000
Total Liabilities	$90,000
Equity	$40,000

better find some new ways to employ his earnings in order to increase earnings above the $4,700 threshold lest his return on equity continues to shrink. In theory, though, if he is retiring debt, he will rid himself of the interest payment on the debt, thus decreasing expenses and potentially increasing earnings. When this happens, return on equity will potentially go up. Until then . . . Joe's a loser.

Similar, Yet Different

It is not too much of a logical leap to first examine a rental property income statement and then to leap to the small business income statement. The similarities between the rental and business income statement are fairly apparent; both are using a standard income statement format. In both you find income, expenses, and a bottom line or net earnings . . . or in other words, the tried and true income statement format: Income minus expenses equals net earnings; everything coming in minus everything going out results in what is left over.

Again, these earnings divided by the equity found on the balance sheet gives us the return on equity, so get to dividing.

A property investor will typically develop the projected income statement in order to check for both cash flow and a healthy rate of return before investing. In many ways, in the context of treating small business as an investment in order to build a small business that Warren Buffett would love, a rental property managed via a property management company is a key cornerstone in understanding the business as an investment. A property managed rental property, in my opinion, is a hybrid between an investment and a business. It is not managed in the traditional, active small business sense, yet it is treated like a business in the income statements (remember that whole income minus expenses equals net income concept?), and the typical investor is seeking cash flow and rate of return, thus making it investment-like.

In another light, a rental property is not bereft of "active" financial statements unlike, let's say, a mutual fund investment. A mutual fund sends a semi-annual and annual report with financial statements, but typically this means very little to the passive investor. (Who cares if the office supply expense for the fund is down if the rate of return was a dismal 1 percent the past quarter?) A rental income statement on the other hand, even under property management, is much more relevant to the property owner. It can be managed, rents can be increased, expenses reduced, and the quality of performance within this financial statement is the difference between receiving a check in the mail or a bill at the end of the month.

Thus, the rental income statement in many ways is the exemplary bridge between a more investment-centered business investment and the small business as a means to receiving a paycheck. The comprehension of the rental property investment parameters, as culled from the projected cash flow income statement, helps to enforce "viewing your small business as an investment."

Return on equity drives the point home.

The entrepreneur who examines for return on equity is not only building a small business that Warren Buffett would love but is truly leveraging his ability to manage the business. Return on equity, bottom line, is a measure of how effectively the equity in the business is being used to generate earnings. The monitoring and management of this number leads to opportunities within the operational statements. Net earnings can be increased through better marketing, higher return business opportunities, and expense reduction. Equity can be utilized in better returning investments. Additionally, the utilization of assets can be monitored via the return on assets formula and capital, or the combination of debt and equity within the business can be measured via the return on capital formula. Although this is not a treatise on ratio management and analysis and Warren Buffett truly seeks return on equity first along with the rest of his recipe as presented in this book, I have put a summary of ratio analysis for small business owners at the end of this chapter. It is not necessary to utilize all of these ratios in order to build a small business that Warren Buffett would love, but they will certainly help in maximizing the potential of the business.

Of Assets, Cash Flow, and Financial Independence

As a side note, in terms of financial independence and return on equity, in the paradigm of Robert Kiyosaki, author of *Rich Dad, Poor Dad*, the business owner is building an asset that should deliver relatively passive cash flow to the income column. The higher the return on investment (the close cousin of return on equity, yet not to be confused), the less capital needed to reach financial independence. An individual with $3,000 a month in expenses and a rate of return of 20 percent can reach financial independence with $180,000, in contrast to a person with the same expense level and a 10 percent rate of return, who will require $360,000.

Here's what our individuals look like

Individual Numero Uno at a 20 percent Rate of Return
$$(.20) \ \$180,000/12 = \$3,000$$

Individual Numero Dos at a 10 percent Rate of Return
$$(.10) \ \$360,000/12 = \$3,000$$

What Warren Wants to See—The Entire Reason We Are Covering This Topic

If Warren Buffett should take a peek at your business's ROE, Table 4.11 shows what he would love to see.

Warren Buffett would prefer to invest in a business with the ROE level and track record of Joe's Hamburger Stand as compared to the paltry performance of Bill's Hamburger Stand. Joe's stand is delivering a much higher return on equity, and if the business has the ability to retain this return (another attribute Warren loves, covered in the next chapter), then the business will grow in value. A business that retains earnings adds to its equity base, and as long as it continues to generate high returns, it should grow in value. Way to go, Joe!

Table 4.11 Warren's Equity Aspirations

This . . .		Not This . . .	
Joe's Hamburger Stand		Bill's Hamburger Stand	
Year	ROE	Year	ROE
1	20%	1	4%
2	25%	2	5%
3	30%	3	5%
4	30%	4	4%
5	35%	5	3%
6	30%	6	5%
7	35%	7	6%
8	40%	8	4%
9	35%	9	4%
10	40%	10	3%

Across the Universe of Investments

For comparative purposes, all else equal, a hamburger stand generating a 32 percent return on equity is superior to a rental property delivering a 26 percent return on equity, and vice versa. In terms of ROE, Joe's is far superior to Bill's, since Joe comes in with a 10-year average of 32 percent versus Bill's anemic 4.3 percent.

Small Business Application

Here's how to wire an ROE framework into your business in order to build a small business Warren Buffett would love.

- If the business is an existing business, run the profit and loss statements for the past 10 years if available (five at the least). If the business is new, then develop a reliable income statement and balance sheet projection for the next five years, keeping in mind the previous warnings about projections (they are made-up guesses).
- Calculate Return on Equity—divide income statement earnings for the year by the end of year equity (assets minus liabilities) as culled from the balance sheet.

- What is the resulting ROE picture? Is it like Joe's or Bill's Hamburger Stand—or perhaps somewhere in between? Ideally, you will see a picture similar to Joe's Hamburger Stand. If not, your job is to become as Joe-like as possible in terms of ROE.

That's not to say that your ROE has to blow the roof off the place and deliver a return in excess of 30 percent. If anything, refer back to the industry average ROE chart in this chapter and use the corresponding industry number as a benchmark, keeping in mind that this is an industry average and, in many ways, ROE should be viewed almost as a separate rate of return. In other words, if your industry's ROE is poor, coming in at low single-digit numbers, then perhaps it is wise to take a gander at industries with ROEs in at least the mid- to upper teens and think about making a switch. As a small business owner turned small business owner-investor, it is important to ask "Why should I invest in a business delivering a 4 percent return on equity when I can invest in a business delivering a 20 percent return on equity?" The second business delivers more efficiently on earnings with the given amount of equity, a very important consideration in the world of Warren Buffett.

Let's go back to our picture of the small business income statement, where you can find the earnings for the top half of the ROE equation and the information necessary to calculate the initial return on investment. See Table 4.12.

And for the ideal ROE picture using Joe's track record as our standard, see Table 4.13.

How to Become Joe-Like

Just to drive home the point, two variables go into the return on equity formula: earnings and equity. Thus, the solution is rather straightforward: Generate as much earnings as possible with as little equity as possible.

The Two Components of Earnings

The component parts of earnings as culled from our income statement are revenues and expenses. Thus, in an easier-said-than-done

Table 4.12   Ye Olde Income Statement for Joe's Hamburger Stand

Initial Investment	$20,000
Revenues	$80,000
COGs	$24,000
Gross Income	$56,000
Expenses	
Payroll	$15,000
Payroll Taxes	$2,550
Supplies	$1,500
Maintenance	$2,700
Marketing/Advertising	$1,400
Car/Travel	$300
Accounting and Legal	$500
Rent	$9,600
Phone	$900
Utilities	$1,500
Insurance	$1,200
Interest	$7,000
Depreciation	$2,500
Total Expenses	$46,650
Net Income	$9,350
Initial Rate of Return	17%

Table 4.13   Joe's ROE

Year	ROE
1	20%
2	25%
3	30%
4	30%
5	35%
6	30%
7	35%
8	40%
9	35%
10	40%

fashion, the way to greater earnings is to *increase revenues and decrease expenses.*

It is highly recommended that you obtain a common size income statement for the industry pertaining to your business so that you can tell if you are off or on. This statement contains "common size" industry ratios for many of the line items found in your income statement, and it serves as an indicator as to whether your expenses are in or out of line with the industry. It's not to say that if you are beating the industry you are golden, since the industry as a whole could be stinking on a certain expense line item, but in general, it should indicate operational areas for managerial improvement. Common size industry reports can be obtained via your local banker or Small Business Development Center. I have included a sample of a common size income statement at the end of this chapter for your merriment.

As for increasing revenues, it is imperative to develop and implement a good marketing plan and a system to track the ROI for marketing spend. (It is not prudent to throw thousands of dollars into a coupon campaign that generates a 4 percent return on investment when the money can be spent elsewhere, say on quirky, acapella group radio jingles asking consumers to spend or else, generating a 10 percent return on investment.)

Liza Minnelli, Dolphins, and Flaming Banana Boats

Circling back to our first Buffett concept, it is also important to examine the business in terms of a consumer monopoly. If your business is the twelfth pizza shop in town and has no distinguishing features (Elvis, tomato sauce spewing volcanoes, Liza Minnelli on a raft in a pool, surrounded by dolphins), the deck is stacked against you, you are swimming against the tide, and someone is about to hurl flaming banana boats at you.

Can This Be Fixed?

If the ROE in the business is flailing at best (or flatlined at worst), as the owner you must ask "Can this be fixed?" Is it possible to increase earnings on top of the existing equity base? Can new revenue generating assets be purchased without using titanic amounts of equity? If not, you should be willing to shift investments in the same manner that Warren Buffett shifted the capital of the original Berkshire Hathaway, the textile manufacturer, into consumer monopoly insurance companies.[4] (GEICO anyone?)

If a shift is necessary, start with earnings and use the income from the sale of assets to purchase businesses fitting the entire Buffett fundamental mold: a consumer monopoly, with a strong track record of earnings, a healthy return on equity, and the ability to retain earnings, with little debt on the balance sheet, possessing the ability to increase prices with inflation, and containing healthy margins relative to other industries.

The lesson here is to not get married to your business if it is in fact a bad business, with flailing underlying economics. You will always be slamming your head against a brick wall of economic reality if you do not heed this advice. This ground-zero of truth truly represents the shift from a small business owner as a pawn to a small business owner as an investor, and although it is easier said than done, making that shift is one more step along the path to building a small business Warren Buffett would love, and to preserving your head.

If the business is new and the "honest" realistic projections do not show the potential for high returns on equity, then look elsewhere. Remember, a business with component pieces that do not fit the Warren Buffett mold is a business that will operate like a bladeless lawn mower.

As always, if you are using projections, keep in mind that projections at best are an accurate forecast and at worst a good guess. If you are thinking of starting a business from scratch, I highly recommend taking a look at an existing business or a franchise business, since the franchisor can provide existing franchise financial data from comparable locations that can be used to paint the financial picture of your franchise start. In other words, the analysis will be grounded in real life numbers, not on a high stakes forecast.

An Afterthought on Financial Ratios

As promised, here is the breakdown on financial ratios pertinent to small business.

Ratios

When potential investors begin the task of analyzing your business for risk and feasibility, they bring experience and expertise to bear on your business plan. What it comes down to is whether or not they

COMMON SIZE STATEMENT

Income Statement Data	06/30/2009	06/30/2010	Industry (4913)
Sales (Income)			
Net Sales	100%	100%	100%
Cost of Sales (COGS)	0%	100%	N/A
Direct Labor	47%	44%	44%
Food Costs	7%	5%	N/A
Gross Profit	39%	38%	N/A
Depreciation	53%	56%	56%
Amortization	0%	0%	3%
Overhead or S,G,& A Expenses	0%	0%	0%
G & A Payroll Expense	95%	68%	40%
Rent	43%	34%	25%
Advertising	10%	9%	6%
Workers Comp	3%	2%	2%
Taxes/Licenses	2%	1%	N/A
Tools/Sm Equipment	0%	N/A	N/A
Supplies	2%	0%	N/A
Maintenance	9%	3%	N/A
Car/Travel	2%	1%	N/A
Acct & Legal	1%	1%	N/A
Phone/Internet/Music	1%	1%	N/A
Utilities	1%	0%	N/A
Insurance	5%	4%	N/A
Equipment Rental	2%	0%	N/A
Bank Charges	0%	0%	N/A
Royalty Fees	0%	1%	N/A
Distribution	5%	2%	N/A
Cash Over/Short	1%	0%	N/A
Comps	0%	0%	N/A
Coupons	3%	3%	N/A
Dues Subscriptions	0%	1%	N/A
Laundry/Uniforms	0%	0%	N/A
Credit Card Fees	2%	2%	N/A
Postal	1%	2%	N/A
Gift Cards	0%	0%	N/A
Outside Services	N/A	1%	N/A
Moving Expenses	0%	0%	N/A
Other Operating Income	1%	0%	N/A
Other Operating Expenses	0%	0%	0%
Operating Profit	0%	0%	10%
Interest Expense	N/A	N/A	4%
Interest-Loans	6%	8%	1%
Other Income	0%	8%	N/A
Other Expenses	0%	0%	0%
Net Profit Before Taxes	0%	0%	0%
Adjusted Net Profit before Taxes	N/A	N/A	3%
EBITDA	N/A	N/A	3%
Taxes Paid	N/A	N/A	7%
Fixed Payroll Taxes	5%	4%	0%
Taxes/Sales	0%	4%	N/A
Extraordinary Gain	0%	N/A	N/A
Extraordinary Loss	0%	0%	0%
Net Income	0%	0%	0%
Net Income	0%	33%	N/A
	N/A	N/A	2%

Figure 4.1 Industry Common Size Statement
Source: ProfitCents, reproduced with permission.

think your business proposal, as presented in your business plan, is feasible. In other words, can your business make money?

Ratio analysis involves crunching ratios using data culled from the financial statements and comparing them to a standard. Knowledge of ratios on your part is akin to learning to speak the language of potential investors. It also gives you a valuable management tool. By tracking your ratios, you can spot trends, strengths, weaknesses, and potential roadblocks.

Liquidity Ratios

The current ratio and the quick ratio are two examples of liquidity ratios. The current ratio is used to determine liquidity of an existing business by dividing current assets by current liabilities. If the current ratio is greater than 1.0, then the business has a chance of being able to pay short-term bills. The larger the number, the better the chance of paying the bills. If that number is less than 1.0, the business may be in rough water. However, decision makers will also take into account industry norms. If the industry standard is 4.0, that current ratio of 1.0 is not nearly as good as it would be in an industry with an average of say, 1.5.

The quick ratio, also called the acid test, is a measurement of liquidity without inventory being calculated and is found by dividing current assets, not including inventory, by current liabilities. Comparing the quick ratio to the current ratio gives decision makers an idea of how dependent liquidity is upon inventory.

Debt Management Ratios

Debt management ratios include the debt ratio and at times the interest earned ratio TIE. The debt ratio is a measure of risk and it shows how well the company's asset supports monetary obligations. The debt ratio is found by dividing total debt, including long-term debt, short-term debt, and current liabilities, by total assets. A high ratio means high risk to potential investors.

The TIE measures how well earnings cover interest and can be found by dividing earnings before interest and taxes by interest. The higher the number the more times earnings can cover interest, thus the safer the investment.

Asset Management Ratios

Inventory turnover and average collection period are both examples of asset management ratios. The inventory turnover ratio measures how often your company gets rid of and restocks an average sized inventory. It is measured by dividing cost of goods sold by inventory. The higher number is better because higher numbers mean you've more quickly gone through your inventory. This means fewer of your business dollars are tied up in inventory. Inventory can cost you in storage, taxes, insurance, and interest as well as time. Inventory and time are not friends. As time passes, inventory can become outdated, unpopular, or even unsafe.

Average collection period measures how long it takes to collect on sales on credit. When you sell on credit there will be a lag time. That lag time is measured by the average collection period. It is found by dividing Accounts Receivable by sales and multiplying the total by 360. Obviously, you want the number to be as small as possible. Ideally, you want it as close to your company's terms of sale as you can get it. If the number exceeds your terms of sales significantly— greater than 30 percent—you show that you are not being as strict with your credit choices as you should be or there is significant customer dissatisfaction.

Profitability Ratios

Profitability ratios include return on sales, return on assets, and return on equity. The return on sales ratio is the most basic measurement of profitability and says something about how well you can keep down costs and expenses. Divide net income by sales and, voilà, you have profitability—at least on paper.

The return on assets ratio similarly says something about how well you use invested assets and is found by dividing net income by total assets.

The return on equity ratio, our important Warren Buffett ratio, builds on the return on assets by taking leverage into account, and it is found by dividing net income by equity. Debt affects return on assets and return on equity, and the two will be close if debt is small. When debt grows large, return on equity is higher than return on assets when the company is doing well, and lower when the company is doing poorly.

Uses of Funds

Most institutions and individuals want to know exactly what you plan on doing with their money. The best place to start with how you will use the funds you are requesting is to provide a summary of your business's financial needs. This is found in the uses of funds section of any standard business plan.

This summary is a simple statement of how the funds will be used and includes one-time capital expenses, one-time working capital needs, and the first six months of your operating expenses or six months of working capital. The second part of this statement will give the sources of funds, including how much the owner is contributing and how much the bank and/or investors are contributing.

Assumptions

The purpose of the assumptions section is to explain to readers how you chose your numbers. Readers turn to this section in order to interpret the biases of the preparer. Assumptions answer the all-important question, why? Why did you do this—so you could double your sales in two years? If readers don't know your reasoning, they cannot make an educated decision as to the validity of your numbers. Your assumptions are yet another chance to convince your readers. With your assumptions in mind, others within your company are better able to meet goals because they know what is behind those goals.

Don't get lazy with this subsection and never assume that any of the numbers are self-explanatory. Discussions about your plan may occur months after you have prepared your numbers, and you might actually forget why, for example, you thought you could double sales within two years.

More Detail on the Ratios

Liquidity Ratios

Current Ratio = Total Current Assets/Total Current Liabilities

Explanation: Generally, this metric measures the overall liquidity position of a company. It is certainly not a perfect barometer, but it is a good one. Watch for big decreases in this number over time. Make sure the accounts listed in "current assets" are collectible. The higher the ratio, the more liquid the company.

Quick Ratio = (Cash + Accounts Receivable)/Total Current Liabilities

Explanation: This is another good indicator of liquidity, although by itself it is not a perfect one. If receivable accounts are included in the numerator, they should be collectible. Look at the length of time the company has to pay the amount listed in the denominator (current liabilities). The higher the number, the stronger the company.

Efficiency

Inventory Days = (Inventory/COGS) * 365

Explanation: This metric shows how much inventory (in days) is on hand. It indicates how quickly a company can respond to market and/or product changes. Not all companies have inventory for this metric. The lower the better.

Accounts Receivable Days = (Accounts Receivable/Sales) * 365

Explanation: This number reflects the average length of time between credit sales and payment receipts. It is crucial to maintaining positive liquidity. The lower the better.

Accounts Payable Days = (Accounts Payable/COGS) * 365

Explanation: This ratio shows the average number of days that lapse between the purchase of material and labor, and payment for them. It is a rough measure of how timely a company is in meeting payment obligations. Lower is normally better.

Profitability

Gross Profit Margin = Gross Profit/Sales

Explanation: This number indicates the percentage of sales revenue that is paid out in direct costs (costs of sales). It is an important statistic that can be used in business planning because it indicates how many cents of gross profit can be generated by each dollar of future sales. Higher is normally better (the company is more efficient).

Net Profit Margin = Adjusted Net Profit before Taxes/Sales

Explanation: This is an important metric. In fact, over time, it is one of the more important barometers that we look at. It measures how many cents of profit the company is generating for every dollar's worth of sales. Track it carefully against industry competitors. This is a very important number in preparing forecasts. The higher the better.

Efficiency

Advertising to Sales = Advertising/Sales

Explanation: This metric shows advertising expense for the company as a percentage of sales.

Rent to Sales = Rent/Sales

Explanation: This metric shows rent expense for the company as a percentage of sales.

G&A Payroll to Sales = G&A Payroll Expense/Sales

Explanation: This metric shows G&A payroll expense for the company as a percentage of sales.

Safety

Interest Coverage Ratio = EBITDA/Interest Expense

Explanation: This ratio measures a company's ability to service debt payments from operating cash flow (EBITDA). An increasing ratio is a good indicator of improving credit quality. The higher the better.

Leverage

Debt-to-Equity Ratio = Total Liabilities/Total Equity

Explanation: This balance sheet leverage ratio indicates the composition of a company's total capitalization—the balance between money or assets owed versus the money or assets owned. Generally, creditors prefer a lower ratio to decrease financial risk, while investors prefer a higher ratio to realize the return benefits of financial leverage.

Debt Leverage Ratio = Total Liabilities/EBITDA

Explanation: This ratio measures a company's ability to repay debt obligations from annualized operating cash flow (EBITDA).

Profitability

Return on Equity = Net Income/Total Equity

Explanation: This measure shows how much profit is being returned on the shareholders' equity each year. It is a vital statistic from the perspective of equity holders in a company. The higher the better.

Return on Assets = Net Income/Total Assets

Explanation: This calculation measures the company's ability to use its assets to create profits. Basically, ROA indicates how many cents of profit each dollar of asset is producing per year. It is quite important, since managers can only be evaluated by looking at how they use the assets available to them. The higher the better.

Efficiency

Fixed Asset Turnover = Sales/Gross Fixed Assets

Explanation: This asset management ratio shows the multiple of annualized sales that each dollar of gross fixed assets is producing. This indicator measures how well fixed assets are "throwing off" sales and is very important to businesses that require significant investments in such assets. Readers should not emphasize this metric when looking at companies that do not possess or require significant gross fixed assets. The higher the number the more effective the company's investments in net property, plant, and equipment are.

Figure 4.2 shows an income statement, balance sheet, and common size statement and key industry financial ratios for industry code 7221, Full-Service Restaurants.

For our current location on the road map, see Figure 4.3.

Small Company Data Table Data Format	Sales < $1,278,814 Median Values	
	US Private Company Data	
	Aggregate	Small Company
Company Count in Analysis	667	157
Income Statement		
Nec Sales	*100%*	*100%*
Gross Profit	63.3%	63.3%
Operating Income	4.8%	4.5%
Net Profit After Tax	2.2%	1.5%
Balance Sheet		
Cash	7.1%	7.1%
Accounts Receivable	0.6%	0%
Inventory	3.4%	2.7%
Total Current Assets	13.3%	11.0%
Total Fixed Assets	52.3%	50.4%
Other Non-Current Assets	34.4%	38.6%
Total Assets	*100%*	*100%*
Accounts Payable	6.6%	2.0%
Total Current Liabilities	40.5%	2965.9%
Total Long-Term Liabilities	17.1%	10.2%
Net Worth	42.4%	−2876.1%
Financial Ratios		
Quick Ratio	0.42	0.28
Current Ratio	0.95	0.66
Current Liabilities to Net Worth	39.0%	16.5%
Current Liabilities to Inventory	639.0%	571.0%
Total Liabilities to Net Worth	86.0%	32.5%
Fixed Assets to Net Worth	80%	36.5%
Collection Period	0.8	0
Inventory Turnover	73.7	67.7
Assets to Sales	35.0%	33.0%
Sales to Working Capital	0.0	−0.9
Accounts Payable to Sales	3.0%	1.0%
Return on Sales	2.0%	2.0%
Return on Assets	5.0%	4.0%
Return on Investment	24.0%	39.5%
Interest Coverage	5.2	3.3

Figure 4.2   Industry Key Financial Ratios
Source: First Research, reproduced with permission.

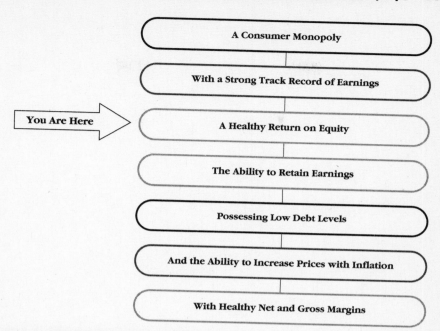

Figure 4.3 Building a Small Business Warren Buffett Would Love the Flowchart

CHAPTER 5

Retained Earnings—The Fuel for the Engine of Compounding Returns

Warren Buffett invests in companies that have the ability to retain and compound earnings at high rates of return. Typically, companies with low plant, equipment, research and development costs will meet this mold.

Warren Buffett leaves his money within these companies so that it may compound at high rates of return. In other words, not only does the business in which Buffett invests retain its earnings and reinvest it back into the business, Warren retains his money within these businesses. He does not withdraw the capital from the investment by selling the stock, nor does he necessarily seek out companies with huge payout through dividends. This paradigm of never selling allows him to snowball his wealth and avoid capital gains tax consequences.

In the universe of small business, small business owners also have the option to leave (or retain) their earnings (if they exist) within the company to compound at high rates of return, if high return reinvestment options are available. If the business does not churn out high rates of return, then the question becomes, is a better investment, one with a higher rate of return, available?

Death of the Compounding Engine

First, the business must have earnings. Secondly, the business must have the ability to generate those earnings using a reasonable base of equity. This results in a high return on equity. Thirdly, the business must have the ability to retain the earnings at the same high rate of return. If a business cannot retain the earnings, then the compounding engine is destroyed.

Let Me Have a Dollar

If I had a magical process for investing capital at a high rate of return, let's say at 20 percent, and you invest $5 with me, at the end of the year I will have made you $1.

You will now be faced with three options:

1. You can take the $1, in which case you can spend it or invest it elsewhere, perhaps in a llama farm.
2. You can leave the $1 with me and allow me to reinvest it for you.
3. Or together, we can use the $1 to buy out existing shareholders.

The first question that should come to mind, if you leave the money with me to reinvest, is "are our children learning," and next, "Will I have the ability to continue generating the 20 percent rate of return?" Then, if you take the $1, what rate of return can you expect to achieve . . . in the llama farm? The answer to the first question is found in two components:

1. The track record of ROE in my business.
2. The historic retained earnings off of my business's balance sheet.

If historically, my business has retained earnings and the ROE has remained strong, averaging 20 percent, then by all appearances the business has the ability to put the $1 to good use, reinvesting it at the high rates of return on equity. If, on the other hand, my business has historically retained earnings (plowed them back into the business for expansion, new business projects, and so on), yet the return on equity has steadily dropped over the years, then it appears that I have poorly allocated retained earnings into low returning investments, and I do not have the capability to effectively expand the business or, at the very least, the core, original business has begun to suck wind. Either way, you will see this as a drop in ROE and perhaps a paltry, anemic ROE track record.

Back to our original options, which truly exist within the context of two scenarios:

1. I have the ability to reinvest the $1 earnings at a 20 percent rate of return.
2. I do not have the ability to reinvest the $1 earnings at a 20 percent rate of return.
3. What would you do with the dollar in each case?

Under scenario 1, if you take the $1 away from me, then in the context of an optimal investing strategy, you must find another investment that generates a 20 percent or greater return in order to beat what I am delivering for you, unless of course you just want to go purchase, let's say, a dozen Krispy Kreme donuts, sit on the couch, and pig out, in which case this is a moot discussion.

Under scenario 2, if my track record is subpar or mediocre at best, then you should take the $1 and invest it elsewhere if you can beat my return. Let's say I generate 4 percent on a regular basis and your local bank is offering a CD paying 5.5 percent. In this scenario, you would be better off (by 1.5 percent) to take your dollar and invest it at the bank. As a matter of fact, I would strongly argue that if the ROE track record of my business has been subpar, then you should give serious consideration to yanking your entire investment and moving it elsewhere, preferably to a company with a strong record of return on equity. This is exactly what Warren Buffett did when he learned that the original Berkshire Hathaway textile business had poor underlying economics.[1] He began buying better businesses.

Of Retained Earnings and Llama Farms

It is possible for a business to have strong return on equity but not the opportunity to reinvest the earnings in profitable expansion ventures. (Remember that whole inability to profitably expand the business bit?) Perhaps the core business is profitable but no new opportunities for reinvestment exist. (None of the llama farms are for sale.) In this case, it is acceptable to distribute the $1 in the form of dividends, in which case the investor (you) will have to go out and do something with the $1. If rate of return and compounding are your concern, then you should seek out investments that ideally match or beat the rate of return you were receiving in the original investment.

The other alternative is to use the earnings to buy out existing shareholders.

In scenario number one, distribution, the business is still a strong business generating a strong return on equity. Management is merely admitting that "Hey, I see no other place to properly allocate the money that will generate a healthy rate of return. Here, you take it."

In scenario number two, let us pretend that along with you, two other folks have invested in our venture. Including me, this gives us a total of four investors, each with a 25 percent share (for simplicity's sake), each entitled to 25 percent of the earnings. If the company has $10 in earnings at the end of the year, each investor gets $2.50.

Back to our retained earnings. What if using the earnings, instead of reinvesting or distributing, we buy out two of the existing shareholders? In this case, you and I each end up with an equal 50 percent share in the business. If the business generates $10 in earnings, then we each will be entitled to $5 in earnings. By buying back shares, we have doubled our earnings per share. Sounds like a good option right?

But . . . We Are Supposed to Be Discussing Small Business, Correct?

The previous discussion on retained earnings certainly applies to your small business. Although you may not necessarily have shareholders, you definitely have the ability to determine your rate of return, ability to retain earnings, and determine whether it is wise to continue do so. If applied, retaining earnings at a high rate of return will help you in building a small business that Warren Buffett would love and to build a compounding engine of wealth.

How to:

- Drag out the old business balance sheet. Preferably, drag out 10 years' worth. If you don't have 10 years of financial statements, then five will do. If you do not have a five-year track record, then use whatever existing track record is available.

- Examine for retained earnings. This will be found in the equity section of the balance sheet, labeled aptly enough, "retained earnings." Has the business had retained earnings over the past number of years? If not, has it even generated earnings? If you have not had earnings, then go directly to Chapter 4, do not pass "GO," do not collect $200. ROE is a moot conversation at this point since the "return" portion of return on equity is found in the earnings and the earnings do not exist! Also, the business must have strong and consistent earnings in order to meet Warren Buffett's second sieve. If it does not have earnings, then he will not love it, will he?
- If you did not have retained earnings but did have earnings, then how were the earnings used? Were they distributed as a payment to the owners, used to buy out existing shareholders or did you buy a box of 100 raspberry filled crullers? If you did distribute the earnings you must ask, were the earnings reinvested in profitable investments or were they merely blown on licorice vines? (Note: I am not saying to not enjoy your money or to not eat donuts. Just keep in mind that Warren Buffett invests in businesses with the ability to reinvest earnings in high returning investments. In context of the Buffett business investment perspective, ideally, you should have the ability to retain your earnings in the business at a high rate of return. Your blow money should come out of your salary, which should be a reasonable salary within the income statement, not a ridiculous amount paid out in order to afford more crullers and licorice vines.)
- Using the track record of return on equity calculated from the last chapter, if you did have retained earnings, did the business consistently deliver on a strong ROE?

In other words, did the business retain earnings (balance sheet) and did it have a return on equity picture similar to Joe's Hamburger Stand? See Table 5.1.

Remember?

Remember also:

$$ROE = Earnings/Equity$$

It is not necessary to have an astronomical ROE in the 30 to 40 percent range, although it certainly is not discouraged if reachable.

Table 5.1   Joe's Return on Equity

Joe's Hamburger Stand

Year	ROE
1	20%
2	25%
3	30%
4	30%
5	35%
6	30%
7	35%
8	40%
9	35%
10	40%

The average return on equity for American corporations is around 12 percent, so anything higher than this can be considered strong. A decent goal is a return on equity of 15 to 20 percent. Anything higher is very superior. Use the industry ROE average table to find the benchmark for your business, again keeping in mind that just because you are meeting the industry average does not mean you have a strong overall return. Remember, a business with a 20 percent ROE is far superior to a business generating an 8 percent return even if the second business is meeting the industry average.

If retained earnings are present within the balance sheet over the years and ROE remained strong throughout the same period, then it is reasonable to say that management was able to profitably allocate the new earnings into new investments.

But the possibility also exists that the return on equity excelled over the years as a result of a reduction in equity (stock buyback), combined with mediocre returns, new investments, that generate paltry earnings. Or perhaps operational expenses spiraled out of control. Let's take a look at this phenomenon.

Looking at a Phenomenon

If I start a business with $20,000 in equity and generate $4,000 in earnings the first year, the return on equity is 20 percent, correct? ($4,000/$20,000). If in the next year the business generates $3,600

Table 5.2 The Stock Buyback Phenomenon

Balance Sheet		
Assets	$100,000	$100,000
Liabilities	$80,000	$82,000
Equity	$20,000	$18,000
Income Statement		
Income	$100,000	$98,600
Expenses	$96,000	$95,000
Earnings	$4,000	$3,600
ROE	20%	20%

in earnings as a result of spiraling expenses, yet the equity level drops to $18,000 due to buybacks, guess what? The return on equity will still be 20 percent! See Table 5.2.

Stock buybacks can be beneficial (remember that you got 50 percent and I got 50 percent after we bought the other two guys out), yet they can also mask the effects of diminishing earnings. Of course, in our paradigm of building a business that Warren Buffett would absolutely fall in love with, our second sieve, "with a strong track record of earnings," will catch this.

Retained Earnings, So What?

Two additional factors regarding retained earnings are very relevant to the small business owner:

1. Compounding
2. Tax bite avoidance

Earnings added to an equity base that is compounding at a high rate of return will snowball the overall value of the business at a great clip, one layer of flakes on top of the other. To illustrate the compounding effect, let us consider a $100 investment that is compounding at 20 percent a year. At the end of one year the $100 investment will grow to $120. Subsequently, $120 dollars compounding at a 20 percent rate of return will result in $144 at the end of year two, and so on.

Table 5.3   Balance Sheet Before Retained Earnings

Assets	$100,000
Liabilities	$80,000
Equity	$20,000

Table 5.4   Balance Sheet After Retained Earnings

Assets	$104,000
Liabilities	$80,000
Equity	$24,000

Analogously, if earnings are retained in a business that generates and continues to generate a high rate of return, the value of the business will compound. In Table 5.4, Ima Business retains $4,000 worth of earnings from the previous year as shown in Table 5.3. Notice that the equity value in the business goes from $20,000 to $24,000. If the business continues to generate earnings on its equity base of 20 percent a year, then the following year, the business, theoretically, should generate $4,800 in earnings. If this is retained at a 20 percent rate, equity will go up to $28,800, and the following year the business will generate $5,760 in earnings (if the ROE remains steady) and so on. Thus, you can see how earnings and return on equity combine to form a compounding powerhouse that lies at the heart of building a small business that Warren Buffett would love.

Taxes, Taxes, Taxes . . . and Death

In addition, distributions result in tax consequences. By leaving the money within the business, distribution taxes can be avoided, whether they are taken out via capital gains, dividend, or income taxes. This is one of the secrets as to how Warren Buffett compounded an initial $105,000 investment into a fortune in excess of $40 billion. His investments have avoided excessive tax bites over the years because he has retained his money within companies that retain their money.

He does not remove the gains because he reasons, "Why the heck would I remove the earnings from the investment? If it is generating a good return, I'll just have to go find another investment generating a good return. It's not as if I am going to go buy a new car. Plus, Uncle Sam is merely going to take his bite on the distribution, eroding my wealth." Remember the whole "let me have a dollar" bit from earlier in the chapter? If I have the ability to generate a 15 percent rate of return on your investment, and I create earnings and give you the option to remove the earnings in order to go buy a spanking new car, or to leave them with me to continue compounding at 15 percent a year, which option would you choose? If you leave the earnings with me they will continue to grow indefinitely, as long as I have the ability to generate a 15 percent rate of return. (Pure Buffett companies with this feature are McDonald's, Coke, and Wal-Mart.) On the other hand, if you purchase the spanking new car, Uncle Sam will first hit you with an income or capital gains tax bite. The second you drive the car off the lot it will be worth approximately 25 percent less, and within five years it will be worth only 30 percent of its original value—if you are lucky.

In other words, if you withdraw $20,000 from the business investment, Uncle Sam will cleave at least $3,000 off the top. The car purchase costs $17,000 and the car will be worth $5,100 at the end of five years. Net overall return: a loss of 75 percent!

This can be compared to the option of leaving the money with me at a 15 percent rate of return per year. At the end of five years, the investment will grow to $40,227. So, compare $5,100 against $40,227, Again, this is how Warren Buffett turned an initial $105,000 investment into a $40 billion fortune, and the money can be used to build a small business that he will love. (Side note: Of course you should have some toys, nice cars included. Just keep in mind the opportunity cost of buying a new car. In our example, we went from $20,000 to $5,100 in the span of five years, not including the expenses of repairs and maintenance, gas and oil.)

Up in the Sky, It's a Plan, It's a Bird, It's . . . Super Buffett

Earnings and high return on equity lie at the heart of Warren Buffet's super-compounding, investing paradigm. In order to build a small business that Warren Buffett would love (and one that will generate tons of value), you also must build a super-compounding engine within the business. The more money left on the table, the more super-compounding the business can do. That's just plain super!

Retained Earnings in Relation to Business Valuation—the Proof in the Pudding

I've touched on building business value briefly and how retained earnings can add to the overall business value, but let us pretend that you are now ready to sell your business (the ultimate goal of every small business, according to some) and let us look back through the lens of valuation briefly and recap the techniques we have already covered in order to put a price tag on the business. (Go ahead and don your imaginary valuation technique glasses now. I'm waiting.)

Comparable Market Analysis

This is the technique similar to the valuation technique that realtors use to put a price tag on a residential piece of real estate. Recent sales prices of business comps are adjusted up or down based on the inferior or superior features of the business with the for-sale sign in order to reach a sales price.

The Asset Approach

Traditionally known as the book value approach, the asset approach sales price is found by subtracting the total liabilities from the total assets. Keep in mind though, if you are buying the business, this approach is assuming you are acquiring all assets and liabilities. Essentially, it is saying you are buying the equity in the business. Also under the asset approach you will find the liquidation approach to valuation, which essentially boils to a price based on a fire sale of the assets.

A more reasonable approach within this context would be to take the market value of the assets and use this as a sales price. For example, let's say that a simple bakery-type business merely has a building and an oven for its assets. (This example is for simplicity's sake only. The business more than likely will also have fixtures, signage, and so on.) If the building is valued at $150,000 and the oven is worth $2,000, then it can be argued that $152,000 is a fair price for the business.

Of course, this approach does not take into consideration intangible items such as customer goodwill and brand loyalty, which can be accounted for in the earnings approach.

The Earnings Approach

Simply put:

The Earnings Approach = Adjusted Earnings/Capitalization Rate

Adjusted earnings are found by adding back to earnings any owner's salary that is over and above what a necessary manager should be paid, adding back any discretionary expense items such as business meals, travel and entertainment, depreciation and amortization expenses, and extraordinary one-time expenses. If the owner is paying himself $100,000 for a job that can be hired out for $50,000, then $50,000 should be added back to the earnings on the income statement for the year. It is also wise to use the average earnings for the previous three to five years in order to come up with a reasonable earnings picture.

It is easy to see that the implementation of a Warren Buffett "strong track record of earnings" will already impact your small business value, since earnings make up the numerator portion of our earnings approach equation.

Capitalization Rates

In one sense capitalization rates can be viewed as the investor's expected rate of return from the business. If a person invests $100,000 and expects a 20 percent rate of return, then the business will have to generate $20,000 a year in earnings. If we flip this around and apply a little bit of algebra, solving for X we can put a price tag on the business. Instead of supplying the amount of investment ($100,000), we solve for the amount of investment (X) needed given the earnings of $20,000 and the desired rate of return of 20 percent.
So . . .

$$(\$100,000).20 = \$20,000$$

Turns into . . .

$$(X).20 = \$20,000$$

Solving for X . . .

$$X = \$20,000 / .20$$

Or . . .

$$X = \$100,000$$

What this means is that, given a level of earnings of $20,000 a year and an expected rate of return or "capitalization rate" of 20 percent, I am willing to pay $100,000 for the investment or business. Later I will walk through a much more sophisticated valuation technique based on Warren Buffett's method using the time value of money. Just understand for now that this is the core of the earnings approach to valuation.

In addition, capitalization rates can be thought of as the rate of return required given the amount of risk within the investment. Generally, the riskier the investment, the higher the required rate of return. Capitalization rates for riskier businesses are therefore higher.

I Like Buckets   What follows is a typical "bucketing" of capitalization rates as found in Steve LeFever's *Profit Mastery*, based on the underlying perceived riskiness of the business model.

- Class 1—10 to 15 percent

These are large-sized businesses, typically with revenues in excess of $10 million.

- Class 2—15 to 20 percent

Class 2 is comprised of businesses with $2 million to $10 million in sales; medium- to large-sized businesses.

- Class 3—20 to 30 percent

Fast growth businesses, small- to medium-sized, with sales ranging from $500,000 to $2 million, make up Class 3.

- Class 4—30 to 50 percent

This class includes small-sized service or retail businesses such as quick service restaurants, hobby shops, and mechanic shops.

- Class 5—40 to 100 percent

Class 5 includes bookkeeping services, consulting firms, web designers, and personal service businesses.

The Formula For a business that falls into Class 2, medium- to large-sized businesses with sales levels of $2 to $10 million, using an average adjusted earnings of $20,000 a year, the formula looks like this:

$$\$20,000/20\% = \$100,000$$

Thus, according to the earnings approach, $100,000 would be a fair price for this business.

One Other Thing to Keep in Mind

In some cases, not all of the assets owned by the business are being used to generate earnings and, therefore, may need to be valued separately. For example, let's say I own and operate a 200-square-foot donut stand that sits on five acres of land. The five acres of land play no part in generating earnings for the business. The land for the most part is not used for parking or signage, it does not host a corn maze, nor is it used for donut rolling contests. In this case, I may wish to price the land separately using the comparable market analysis valuation method for land. This value can be added to the earnings value for the 200-square-foot donut stand for a total value, or possibly it can be sold separately.

How Warren Buffett Determines the Price

Now let us examine how the big chief determines price. Again, leading up to this point on our "Building a Small Business Warren Buffett Would Love the Flowchart,™" we have defined a consumer monopoly company that generates strong and consistent earnings, with a high return on equity and the ability to retain earnings. At this point on the map we are concerned with the retained earnings adding value to the small business. (See Figure 5.1.)

Warren Buffett invests in businesses that, via the ability to consistently retain earnings at a high return on equity, will exponentially grow in value over time. In order to build a business that Warren

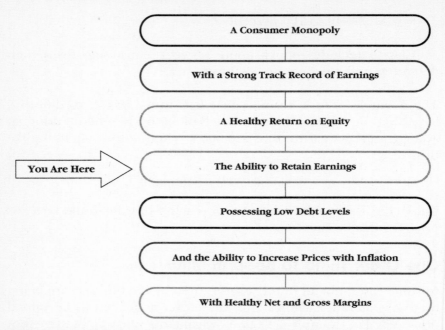

Figure 5.1   Building a Small Business Warren Buffett Would Love Flowchart

Buffett would love, and create wealth, you must have the ability to increase the value of your business over time and use Warren Buffett's methodology for determining price in order to measure your business' value.

What follows is how Warren Buffett uses the return on equity of a business along with the current per share shareholder's equity value in order to project a future trading price and rate of return. (See Table 5.5.)

Explanation

First, any yield attributed to the payout of dividends is subtracted from the average 10-year return on equity in order to reach the true rate of equity growth of shareholder's equity, or in other words, the true return on equity. The reasoning behind this calculation is to

Table 5.5 Determining Value Using Equity Share Value

	MCD	KO	DIS
Average ROE	21.1%	32.2%	9.1%
Average Annual Dividend Yield	3.0%	3.0%	0.9%
True Equity Rate of Growth of Shareholder's Equity	18.1%	29.2%	8.2%
Total Shares (in Millions)	1,080	2,295	1,899
Total Equity (in Millions)	15,458	31,003	37,519
Per-Share Shareholder's Equity Value	$14.31	$13.51	$19.76
N	10	10	10
I/Y	18.1%	29.2%	8.2%
PV	$14.31	$13.51	$19.76
CPT FV—Future Per-Share Value of Company's Shareholder's Equity	$75.82	$175.37	$43.30
Projected Future EPS	$16.03	$56.50	$3.94
Average 10-year P/E	20	23	25
Company's Per Share Projected Future 2020 Trading Price	$320.64	$1,299.60	$98.41
PV (Company's Current Price)	$75.78	$65.22	$42.97
FV	$320.64	$1,299.60	$98.41
N	10	10	10
CPT I/Y (Company's Projected Annual Compounding Rate of Return)	15.5%	34.9%	8.6%
Projected Future Trading Price of the Company's Stock	$320.64	$1,299.60	$98.41
Current Trading Price	$75.78	$65.22	$42.97

exclude dividends from our subsequent compounding calculations, since they are paid out and truly play no part in the future compounding of the equity.

Next, we find the total shares outstanding and total equity in the company from the balance sheet (easy to obtain from Morningstar .com for public companies) and divide the total equity by the number of shares outstanding in order to determine the per-share shareholder's equity value. This figure is not necessarily the share price, but it represents the amount of equity in the company that each shareholder can technically claim per share.

Our next step is to determine the future value of the company's per-share equity value, using the true rate of growth of our equity, and the current per-share equity values—in this case, $14.31, $13.51, and $19.76 for McDonald's, Coke, and Disney respectively. These calculations can easily be computed using a BAII Plus business calculator and by plugging in, in the case of McDonald's, 10 for N or the number of years, 18.1 percent for I/Y or the interest rate, and $14.31 for the present value.

Hit "compute," "FV" to find the future value, and you should get $320.64 for McDonald's. What this tells us is that if McDonald's continues to generate an average 18.1 percent return on equity, in 10 years the equity value per share should grow to $75.82. (See why predictability is so important? We could not count on any McDonald's reliability going forward 10 years if some degree of consistency was not present in their history.)

From this result, we can use the full 21 percent return on equity for McDonald's, multiplied by the future $75.82 equity share value, in order to determine that the company should have $16.03 in earnings per share. (Remember, the "return" portion of return on equity equates to earnings. By simply multiplying the historic average return on equity by the future per-share equity value, we should be able to determine the future earnings per share.) We then multiply this result by the average 10-year historic price to earnings ratio (again, Morningstar.com is invaluable for this information) in order to determine the theoretical future share price. If price divided by earnings results in the P/E ratio, then using some simple algebra, solving for P should give us the price.

$$Price/Earnings = P/E \text{ Ratio}$$

$$Price/\$16.03 = 20$$

$$\$16.03 \ (Price/\$16.03) = 20 * \$16.03$$

$$Price = \$320.64$$

Breaking out our BA II Plus calculator again, we plug in the current price of MCD, (at the time of this writing $75.78), $320.64 for the future value, 10 for N or the number of years, and compute the I/Y, which gives us the company's projected annual compounding rate of return. In McDonald's case it is 15.52 percent:

Projected Future Trading Price: $320.64
Current Trading Price: $75.78
Projected Annual Compounding Rate of Return: 15.52%

Always remember as well that the price you pay determines your rate of return, similar to the old adage for buying a house: "You make your money when you buy." Similar, yet different. So, if you waited to buy McDonald's at a price of $65, then your rate of return would go up to 17.3 percent.

Is This Good or Bad?

You tell me. In a mutual fund I can expect to achieve a 10 to 11 percent return a year over the long haul. CDs and T-bills are paying between 3 and 5 percent, and my fourplex averages about a 10 percent rate of return. In my opinion, 15.52 percent is a great return. Coke and Disney have projected returns of 34.88 percent (whoa!) and 8.64 percent respectively.

Is This Reliable?

You've seen the reasoning for picking companies that have reliable historic indicators: a consumer monopoly; staple, invaluable branding; a strong track record of consistent earnings with a consistent high return on equity. All roads lead to Rome, and in this case, the roads have led us here (in a buggy with Warren Buffett in the passenger's seat), and this is how Warren Buffett determines the future value of a stock and his expected rate of return.

It is always nice to have some verification though, especially in the realm of "if it sounds too good to be true." Coke has a 34.88 percent projected return—good golly! This sounds really great, but let us take a look at Buffett's second valuation technique and see if we can get some corroboration around this spectacular return.

But first . . .

How the Heck Does This Apply to My Small Business?

Okay, okay, I know. We are here to talk about small business, not stock investments. Here is how the earlier calculations can be applied to your small business.

Return on equity can be found simply by dividing the year-end earnings, or net income after tax, from the income statement, by the amount of equity in the business found on the balance sheet. (Remember, assets minus liabilities equals equity.) If the business has not been open for 10 years, then you may want to use projections to make up the difference, keeping in mind all of my feelings about projections. For example, if the business has been operating for five years, you may want to project out five years' worth of earnings in order to have a full 10-year set. If it is a start-up, then you will be relying solely on projections. (Tread softly here.) If you pay dividends to shareholders, then just as in the Buffett stock methodology, subtract out this yield.

Now, more than likely, your company does not have shares. I don't believe most small businesses do, from my experience. If it does, then continue on with the calculations as shown above on a per-share basis. If you do not have shares, then simply use the total current equity value in the business in order to determine the growth of the overall equity, which will tell you the resultant net worth of the business. For example, if you have $100,000 equity in the business and a 15 percent return on equity, using our old reliable BA II Plus, the inputs will be as follows:

$$N = 10$$

$$I/Y = 15\%$$

$$PV = \$100,000$$

Hit "CPT FV" and you will find that the future value of the business's equity is $404,556. You can now multiply this number by the 10-year return on equity of 15 percent and determine that the future yearly earnings at the end of year 10 for the business will be $60,683. At this point, if your business does not have shares outstanding, it is not possible to continue on with the calculations, since a price to earnings ratio does not exist. If the business has shares, then continue on with the calculations in the previous example in order to determine the future trading price and annual compounding rate of return.

What you do know, though, is very important and relevant in building a small business that Warren Buffett would love. You know that your business on average delivers a 15 percent return on equity;

the future net worth of the business will be $404,556; and the earnings will be $60,683. If the earnings average $55,000 over the three years leading up to year 10, and your cap rate is 15 percent, using the earnings valuation approach, a fair price tag for the business will be $366,667 ($55,000/15%).

Given this information, is 15 percent a good compounding rate given your other investment options? Does $366,667 to $404,556 sound like a fair price for your business 10 years down the road?

Technique Numero Dos

In the last technique (Warren Buffett valuation technique Numero Uno), we saw how he uses the return on equity and current per-share shareholder's equity value in order to project a future trading price and rate of return. In a second, validating, valuation technique, we see how he uses the earnings per share growth rate in order to project a future price and rate of return. (Ladies and gentleman, please start your BA II Plus engines.)

Table 5.6 Determining Value Using Historic EPS

	MCD	KO	DIS
PV (EPS 2000 or 1999)	$1.46	$1.33	$0.30
FV (EPS 2010 or 2009)	$4.58	$2.93	$2.07
N	10	10	10
CPT I/Y (Per-Share Annual Compounding Growth Rate for 2000 to 2010)	12.1%	8.2%	21.3%
PV (EPS 2010)	$4.58	$2.93	$2.07
I/Y	0.1211	0.0822	0.2131
N	10	10	10
CPT FV (Projected EPS for 2020)	$14.37	$6.46	$14.29
Average 10-year P/E	20	23	25
Company's Per-Share Projected Future 2020 Trading Price	$287.40	$148.58	$357.25
PV (Company's Current Price)	$75.78	$65.22	$42.97
FV	287.4	148.58	357.25
N	10	10	10
CPT I/Y (Company's Projected Annual Compounding Rate of Return using Historic EPS)	14.26%	8.58%	23.59%

Explanation

In the second Warren Buffett valuation technique, our corroborating method, historic earnings-per-share numbers are used for each of our respective companies from 10 years ago as our present value, and the most recent, complete earnings-per-share is used for the future value. (Note: based on data availability, I used the years 2000 and 2010 in some cases, and 1999 and 2009 in others.) By plugging in these numbers (yes, again we call on our trusty BAII Plus) and using 10 for N, I determined the per-share annual compounding growth rates for each of the companies—in this case, 12.1, 8.2, and 21.3 percent for McDonald's, Coke, and Disney respectively.

Using these numbers and the most recent earnings-per-share numbers, we can now project the future value of the earnings per share at the end of 10 years and, by using the P/E ratio, we can also determine the future 2020 trading price.

Simply multiply the average 10-year P/E by the projected EPS to arrive at a future trading price—in the case of our examples, $287.40, $148.58, and $357.25 for McDonald's, Coke, and Disney respectively. Plugging in the current stock price for the present value and the projected future trading price for the future value in our BA II Plus calculator, and solving for I/Y over a 10-year period, tells us the projected annual rate of return using the historic earnings per share. In this case, it is 14.26, 8.58, and 23.59 percent.

Now we have some corroborating evidence for the price and the return, which is always nice to have.

Let us compare . . .

Using the per-share equity methodology, we found that McDonald's *should* be trading at $320.64 in the future. Using the historic

Table 5.7   Our Valuation Summary

	MCD	KO	DIS
Projected 2020 Trading Range Using Per-Share Equity	$320.64	$1,299.60	$98.41
Projected 2020 Trading Range Using Historic EPS	$287.40	$148.58	$357.25
Average	$304.02	$724.09	$227.83
Projected Rate of Return Using Per-Share Equity	15.5%	34.9%	8.6%
Projected Rate of Return Using Historic EPS	14.3%	8.6%	23.6%
Average	14.9%	21.7%	16.1%

earnings per share, we arrived at $287.40. Not bad; the range is fairly close. The average of these two figures is a future trading price of $304.02 for McDonald's. For the rate of return we found 15.5 percent and 14.3 percent, leading to an average 14.9 percent. I feel confident in these numbers. How about you?

For Coke, we came up with ridiculous ranges of $148.58 to $1,299.60 for the price and 8.6 percent to 34.9 percent for the rate of return, resulting in averages of $724.09 and 21.7 percent respectively. I would put zero confidence in these results since the ranges are so disparate. I might go back and double-check the numbers and explore why the numbers are so extreme. Off the bat, you can see that Coke has had a very high historic return on equity of 32 percent, which leads to our "big" result in the per-share equity analysis. Can they keep this up? Well, they are Coke after all, and no matter where you are at this moment, barring the North Pole, I bet a Coke is about 100 yards away. Additionally, if you ever tire of drinking Coke, you can always switch to orange juice, fruit juice, or water, but you still may be drinking Coke—Minute Maid, Spirit of Georgia, Dasani.[2]

How the Heck Do I Apply the Historic Earnings Per-Share Method to My Small Business?

Good question. Here's how.

Start by finding your historic and most recent earnings data. This will most likely not be on a per-share basis but that is okay; just use the year-end earnings from 10 years ago and the most recent, complete yearly earnings. Plug these figures into your BA II Plus calculator as the present value and the future value; use 10 for the number of years; and compute I/Y. This result tells you the annual compounding growth rate of your earnings. In other words, on average, at what rate have your earnings been growing? For example, a company that had $50,000 in earnings 10 years ago and $100,000 last year will have an annual compounding earnings growth rate of 7.18 percent. In McDonald's case, the growth rate is 12.11 percent.

Next, use this growth rate, along with the most recent year's complete earnings picture—in our example $100,000—to find the projected earnings 10 years out. In our case, using $100,000 for the present value, 7.18 percent for I/Y, and 10 for N, we compute the future value and find that in 10 years our business should have earnings of $200,050. Again, the importance of reliability is evident in this calculation, which entirely depends on the business's ability to continue growing earnings at a 7.18 percent rate. Predictability is key.

At this point, again, without a price-to-earnings ratio, it is not possible to continue the calculations, but you have obtained valuable information from the above calculations.

You know that earnings are growing at 7.18 percent and, if this rate continues, you should have earnings of $200,050 in 10 years. You can compare this number to the earnings results found in the equity share value technique and use this to determine a valuation range. For example, let's say that in the equity share value technique, we found that earnings are projected to be at $80,000 a year, and in the historic EPS method earnings are projected to be at $100,000 a year. A cap rate of 15 percent will give us a business value range of $533,333 to $666,667.

$$\$80,000/.15 = \$533,333$$

$$\$100,000/.15 = \$666,667$$

You now have the ability to project a future potential sales price of your business using two robust Warren Buffett valuation techniques. Congratulations! Extend hand, reach around to back, commence patting.

Valuation as It Relates to Retained Earnings

Just to drive the point home, as it relates to the topic of the chapter, retained earnings:

Retained earnings add to equity.

ROE = Earnings/Equity.

In the example of a hamburger stand reinvesting the earnings into a second location, let us say that the owner purchases a new grill, new fixtures, and booths, signage, tables, and supplies.

- Under the asset approach, saleable assets have been added to the balance sheet.
- Under the comparable market analysis approach, a potential second location has been added.
- Under the earnings approach, ideally, earnings should increase. Let's say, for example, the owner doubles earnings

from $100 a year to $200 a year. If the capitalization rate for his business is 20 percent, then the value of the business will go from $500 to $1,000.

- Under the Warren Buffett approach to valuation, retained earnings add to the equity base. If the return on equity level is maintained with the new equity base, then per shareholder's equity value will grow under technique number one, even if there is only one shareholder in your business. Under technique number two, the earnings level of the business as a whole will potentially increase, adding value to the business, similar to the earnings approach to valuation.

Low Research and Design, Low Required Investments in Maintenance and Upkeep . . . Low I Tell You, Low

One last key point that is very important to keep in mind when evaluating your existing or start-up business in terms of retained earnings and building a small business that Warren Buffett would love: Make sure the business does not have significant yearly expenses in research and development or repairs and maintenance.

The reason why: A business that has to continually nurse large expenditures in this area will always be hampered as to earnings. It's as if the business has to drive through two major, expense draining toll booths on the income statement before arriving at the earnings bottom line. This will always work against the business as opposed to companies like Coke (no one is spending time in the R&D lab reinventing the formula for Coke); Fruit of the Loom is not reengineering the t-shirt; and Hershey's is not reinventing the recipe for chocolate. Companies with a large R&D feature and heavy expenses in maintenance and upkeep (think automotive companies that have to constantly retool plants for next year's models and replace depreciated equipment) do not have the natural economics needed to pass more along to the bottom line. Companies that do not have this burden have a greater proclivity for large earnings, greater return on equity, bigger retained earnings and the love of Warren Buffett. See Tables 5.8, 5.9, 5.10, 5.11, 5.12, 5.13, 5.14, and 5.15. Please also see the flowchart in Figure 5.2.

Table 5.8 Coca-Cola Co (KO) Income Statement

USD in Millions Except Per Share Data

Fiscal year ends in December	2001-12	2002-12	2003-12	2004-12	2005-12	2006-12	2007-12	2008-12	2009-12	2010-12	TTM
Revenue	$20,092	$19,564	$21,044	$21,962	$23,104	$24,088	$28,857	$31,944	$30,990	$35,119	$38,111
Cost of Revenue	$6,044	$7,105	$7,762	$7,638	$8,195	$8,164	$10,406	$11,374	$11,088	$12,693	$14,101
Gross profit	$14,048	$12,459	$13,282	$14,324	$14,909	$15,924	$18,451	$20,570	$19,902	$22,426	$24,010
Operating Expenses											
Sales, General, and Administrative	$8,696	$7,001	$8,061	$8,626	$8,824	$9,616	$11,199	$11,774	$11,358	$13,158	$14,533
Other Operating Expenses								$350	$313	$819	$932
Total Operating Expenses	$8,696	$7,001	$8,061	$8,626	$8,824	$9,616	$11,199	$12,124	$11,671	$13,977	$15,465

Operating Income	$5,352	$5,458	$5,221	$5,698	$6,085	$6,308	$7,252	$8,446	$8,231	$8,449	$8,545
Interest Expense	$289	$199	$178	$196	$240	$220	$456	$438	$355	$733	$761
Other Income (Expense)	$607	$240	$452	$720	$845	$490	$1,077	($569)	$1,070	$6,527	$6,791
Income before Taxes	$5,670	$5,499	$5,495	$6,222	$6,690	$6,578	$7,873	$7,439	$8,946	$14,243	$14,575
Provision for Income Taxes	$1,691	$1,523	$1,148	$1,375	$1,818	$1,498	$1,892	$1,632	$2,040	$2,384	$2,429
Other Income									($82)	($50)	($51)
Net Income from Continuing Operations	$3,979	$3,976	$4,347	$4,847	$4,872	$5,080	$5,981	$5,807	$6,824	$11,809	$12,095
Cumulative Effect of Accounting Changes	($10)	($926)									
Net Income	$3,969	$3,050	$4,347	$4,847	$4,872	$5,080	$5,981	$5,807	$6,824	$11,809	$12,095

(Continued)

105

Table 5.8 (Continued)

Fiscal year ends in December	2001-12	2002-12	2003-12	2004-12	2005-12	2006-12	2007-12	2008-12	2009-12	2010-12	TTM
Net Income Available to Common Shareholders	$3,969	$3,050	$4,347	$4,847	$4,872	$0	$5,981	$5,807	$6,824	$11,809	$12,095
Earnings per Share											
Basic	$1.60	$1.23	$1.77	$2.00	$2.04	$2.16	$2.59	$2.51	$2.95	$5.12	$5.25
Diluted	$1.60	$1.23	$1.77	$2.00	$2.04	$2.16	$2.57	$2.49	$2.93	$5.06	$5.18
Weighted Average Shares Outstanding											
Basic	2,487	2,478	2,459	2,426	2,392	2,348	2,313	2,315	2,314	2,308	2,305
Diluted	2,487	2,483	2,462	2,429	2,393	2,350	2,331	2,336	2,329	2,333	2,334

Source: Morningstar.com.

Table 5.9 Coca-Cola Co (KO) Balance Sheet

USD in Millions Except Per Share Data

Fiscal year ends in December	2001-12	2002-12	2003-12	2004-12	2005-12	2006-12	2007-12	2008-12	2009-12	2010-12
Assets										
Current Assets										
Cash										
Cash and Cash Equivalents	$1,866	$2,126	$3,362	$6,707	$4,701	$2,440	$4,093	$4,701	$7,021	$8,517
Short-Term Investments	$68	$219	$120	$61	$66	$150	$215	$278	$2,192	$2,820
Total Cash	$1,934	$2,345	$3,482	$6,768	$4,767	$2,590	$4,308	$4,979	$9,213	$11,337
Receivables	$1,882	$2,097	$2,091	$2,171	$2,281	$2,587	$3,317	$3,090	$3,758	$4,430
Inventories	$1,055	$1,294	$1,252	$1,420	$1,424	$1,641	$2,220	$2,187	$2,354	$2,650
Prepaid Expenses	$2,300	$1,616	$1,571	$1,735	$1,778	$1,623	$2,260	$1,920	$2,226	$3,162
Total Current Assets	$7,171	$7,352	$8,396	$12,094	$10,250	$8,441	$12,105	$12,176	$17,551	$21,579
Non-Current Assets										
Property, Plant, and Equipment										

(Continued)

Table 5.9 (Continued)

Fiscal year ends in December	2001-12	2002-12	2003-12	2004-12	2005-12	2006-12	2007-12	2008-12	2009-12	2010-12
Gross Property, Plant, and Equipment	$7,105	$9,001	$9,622	$10,149	$10,139	$11,911	$14,444	$14,400	$16,467	$21,706
Accumulated Depreciation	($2,652)	($3,090)	($3,525)	($4,058)	($4,353)	($5,008)	($5,951)	($6,074)	($6,906)	($6,979)
Net Property, Plant, and Equipment	$4,453	$5,911	$6,097	$6,091	$5,786	$6,903	$8,493	$8,326	$9,561	$14,727
Equity and Other Investments								$5,779	$6,755	$7,585
Goodwill						$1,403	$4,256	$4,029	$4,224	$11,665
Intangible Assets	$2,579	$3,553	$3,989	$3,836	$3,821	$3,732	$7,963	$8,476	$8,604	$15,244
Other Long-Term Assets	$8,214	$7,685	$8,860	$9,306	$9,570	$9,484	$10,452	$1,733	$1,976	$2,121
Total Non-Current Assets	$15,246	$17,149	$18,946	$19,233	$19,177	$21,522	$31,164	$28,343	$31,120	$51,342
Total Assets	$22,417	$24,501	$27,342	$31,327	$29,427	$29,963	$43,269	$40,519	$48,671	$72,921

Liabilities and Stockholders' Equity

Liabilities

Current Liabilities

Short-Term Debt	$3,899	$2,655	$2,906	$6,021	$4,546	$3,268	$6,052	$6,531	$6,800	$9,376
Accounts Payable	$3,679	$3,692	$4,058	$4,283	$4,493	$929	$1,380	$1,370	$1,410	$1,887
Taxes Payable								$252	$264	$273
Accrued Liabilities	$851	$994	$922	$667	$797	$4,693	$5,793	$4,835	$5,247	$6,972
Total Current Liabilities	$8,429	$7,341	$7,886	$10,971	$9,836	$8,890	$13,225	$12,988	$13,721	$18,508

Non-Current Liabilities

Long-Term Debt	$1,219	$2,701	$2,517	$1,157	$1,154	$1,314	$3,277	$2,781	$5,059	$14,041
Deferred Taxes	$442	$399	$337	$450	$352	$608	$1,890	$877	$1,580	$4,261
Minority Interest									$547	$314
Other Long-Term Liabilities	$961	$2,260	$2,512	$2,814	$1,730	$2,231	$3,133	$3,401	$2,965	$4,794
Total Non-Current Liabilities	$2,622	$5,360	$5,366	$4,421	$3,236	$4,153	$8,300	$7,059	$10,151	$23,410

(Continued)

Table 5.9 (Continued)

Fiscal year ends in December	2001-12	2002-12	2003-12	2004-12	2005-12	2006-12	2007-12	2008-12	2009-12	2010-12
Total Liabilities	$11,051	$12,701	$13,252	$15,392	$13,072	$13,043	$21,525	$20,047	$23,872	$41,918
Stockholders' Equity										
Common Stock	$873	$873	$874	$875	$877	$878	$880	$880	$880	$880
Additional Paid-In Capital	$3,520	$3,857	$4,395	$4,928	$5,492	$5,983	$7,378	$7,966	$8,537	$10,057
Retained Earnings	$23,443	$24,506	$26,687	$29,105	$31,299	$33,468	$36,235	$38,513	$41,537	$49,278
Treasury Stock	($13,682)	($14,389)	($15,871)	($17,625)	($19,644)	($22,118)	($23,375)	($24,213)	($25,398)	($27,762)
Accumulated Other Comprehensive Income	($2,788)	($3,047)	($1,995)	($1,348)	($1,669)	($1,291)	$626	($2,674)	($757)	($1,450)
Total Stockholders' Equity	$11,366	$11,800	$14,090	$15,935	$16,355	$16,920	$21,744	$20,472	$24,799	$31,003
Total Liabilities and Stockholders' Equity	$22,417	$24,501	$27,342	$31,327	$29,427	$29,963	$43,269	$40,519	$48,671	$72,921

Source: Morningstar.com.

Table 5.10 McDonald's Corporation (MCD) Income Statement

USD in Millions Except Per Share Data

Fiscal year ends in December	2001-12	2002-12	2003-12	2004-12	2005-12	2006-12	2007-12	2008-12	2009-12	2010-12	TTM
Revenue	$14,870	$15,406	$17,140	$19,065	$20,460	$21,586	$22,787	$23,522	$22,745	$24,075	$24,576
Cost of Revenue	$7,353	$7,668	$8,532	$9,377	$14,136	$14,602	$14,881	$14,883	$13,953	$14,437	$14,758
Gross Profit	$7,517	$7,737	$8,608	$9,688	$6,324	$6,984	$7,905	$8,639	$8,792	$9,637	$9,818
Operating Expenses											
Sales, General, and Administrative	$4,563	$4,791	$5,244	$5,706	$2,221	$2,338	$2,367	$2,356	$2,234	$2,333	$2,351
Restructuring, Merger, and Acquisition											
Other Operating Expenses	$257	$833	$532	$441	$82	($38)	($89)	($159)	($283)	($169)	($158)
Total Operating Expenses	$4,820	$5,624	$5,776	$6,148	$2,303	$240	$1,748	$2,196	$1,951	$2,164	$2,193
Operating Income	$2,697	$2,113	$2,832	$3,540	$4,022	$2,539	$4,026	$6,443	$6,841	$7,473	$7,625
Interest Expense	$452	$374	$388	$358	$356	$4,445	$3,879	$523	$473	$451	$460
Other Income (Expense)	$85	($77)	($98)	$20	$36	$402	$410	$238	$119	($22)	($23)
Income before Taxes	$2,330	$1,662	$2,346	$3,202	$3,702	$123	$103	$6,158	$6,487	$7,000	$7,142
						$4,166	$3,572				

(Continued)

Table 5.10 (Continued)

Fiscal year ends in December	2001-12	2002-12	2003-12	2004-12	2005-12	2006-12	2007-12	2008-12	2009-12	2010-12	TTM
Provision for Income Taxes	$693	$670	$838	$924	$1,099	$1,293	$1,237	$1,845	$1,936	$2,054	$2,077
Net Income from Continuing Operations	$1,637	$992	$1,508	$2,278	$2,602	$2,873	$2,335	$4,313	$4,551	$4,946	$5,066
Net Income from Discontinuing Ops						$671	$60				
Cumulative Effect of Accounting Changes		($99)	($37)								
Net Income	$1,637	$894	$1,471	$2,278	$2,602	$3,544	$2,395	$4,313	$4,551	$4,946	$5,066
Net Income Available to Common Shareholders	$1,637	$894	$1,471	$2,278	$2,602	$3,544	$2,395	$4,313	$4,551	$4,946	$5,066
Earnings per Share											
Basic	$1.27	$0.70	$1.16	$1.81	$2.06	$2.87	$2.02	$3.83	$4.17	$4.64	$4.79
Diluted	$1.25	$0.70	$1.15	$1.79	$2.04	$2.83	$1.98	$3.76	$4.11	$4.58	$4.73
Weighted Average Shares Outstanding											
Basic	1,290	1,273	1,270	1,260	1,260	1,234	1,188	1,127	1,092	1,066	1,058
Diluted	1,309	1,282	1,276	1,274	1,274	1,252	1,212	1,146	1,107	1,080	1,071

Source: Morningstar.com.

Table 5.11 McDonald's Corporation (MCD) Balance Sheet

USD in Millions Except Per Share Data

Fiscal year ends in December	2001-12	2002-12	2003-12	2004-12	2005-12	2006-12	2007-12	2008-12	2009-12	2010-12
Assets										
Current Assets										
Cash										
Cash and Cash Equivalents	$418	$330	$493	$1,380	$4,260	$2,136	$1,981	$2,063	$1,796	$2,387
Total Cash	$418	$330	$493	$1,380	$4,260	$2,136	$1,981	$2,063	$1,796	$2,387
Receivables	$882	$855	$734	$746	$796	$904	$1,054	$931	$1,060	$1,179
Inventories	$106	$112	$129	$148	$147	$149	$125	$112	$106	$110
Prepaid Expenses	$414	$418	$529	$585	$646	$436	$422	$412	$454	$692
Total Current Assets	$1,819	$1,715	$1,885	$2,858	$5,850	$3,625	$3,582	$3,518	$3,416	$4,368
Non-Current Assets										
Property, Plant, and Equipment										
Gross Property, Plant, and Equipment	$24,106	$26,219	$28,740	$30,508	$29,897	$31,810	$32,204	$31,152	$33,440	$34,482

(Continued)

Table 5.11 (Continued)

Fiscal year ends in December	2001-12	2002-12	2003-12	2004-12	2005-12	2006-12	2007-12	2008-12	2009-12	2010-12
Accumulated Depreciation	($6,816)	($7,635)	($8,816)	($9,805)	($9,989)	($10,964)	($11,219)	($10,898)	($11,909)	($12,422)
Net Property, Plant, and Equipment	$17,290	$18,583	$19,925	$20,703	$19,908	$20,846	$20,985	$20,254	$21,532	$22,061
Equity and Other Investments								$1,222	$1,213	$1,335
Goodwill					$1,951	$2,209	$2,301	$2,237	$2,425	$2,586
Intangible Assets	$1,420	$1,560	$1,665	$1,828						
Other Long-Term Assets	$2,006	$2,112	$2,050	$2,448	$2,280	$2,344	$2,524	$1,230	$1,639	$1,625
Total Non-Current Assets	$20,715	$22,255	$23,640	$24,980	$24,139	$25,398	$25,810	$24,944	$26,809	$27,607
Total Assets	$22,534	$23,970	$25,525	$27,838	$29,989	$29,024	$29,392	$28,462	$30,225	$31,975
Liabilities and Stockholders' Equity										
Liabilities										
Current Liabilities										

Short-Term Debt	$362	$276	$388	$862	$1,203	$18	$1,991	$32	$18	$8
Accounts Payable	$690	$636	$577	$714	$689	$834	$624	$620	$636	$944
Taxes Payable								$253	$480	$387
Accrued Liabilities	$996	$1,303	$1,227	$1,368	$1,343	$1,654	$1,635	$1,633	$1,855	$1,586
Other Current Liabilities	$201	$208	$294	$576	$801	$502	$248			
Total Current Liabilities	$2,248	$2,422	$2,486	$3,520	$4,036	$3,008	$4,498	$2,538	$2,989	$2,925
Non-Current Liabilities										
Long-Term Debt	$8,556	$9,704	$9,342	$8,357	$8,937	$8,416	$7,310	$10,186	$10,560	$11,497
Deferred Taxes Liabilities	$1,112	$1,004	$1,015	$782	$977	$1,066	$961	$945	$1,279	$1,332
Other Long-Term Liabilities	$1,130	$560	$700	$977	$892	$1,075	$1,342	$1,410	$1,363	$1,587
Total Non-Current Liabilities	$10,798	$11,267	$11,057	$10,116	$10,806	$10,557	$9,613	$12,541	$13,202	$14,416
Total Liabilities	$13,046	$13,690	$13,543	$13,636	$14,843	$13,566	$14,112	$15,079	$16,191	$17,341

(Continued)

Table 5.11 (Continued)

Fiscal year ends in December	2001-12	2002-12	2003-12	2004-12	2005-12	2006-12	2007-12	2008-12	2009-12	2010-12
Stockholders' Equity										
Common Stock	$17	$17	$17	$17	$17	$17	$17	$17	$17	$17
Additional Paid-In Capital	$1,591	$1,747	$1,838	$2,186	$2,798	$3,445	$4,227	$4,600	$4,854	$5,196
Retained Earnings	$18,608	$19,204	$20,172	$21,756	$23,516	$25,846	$26,462	$28,954	$31,271	$33,812
Treasury Stock	($8,912)	($8,988)	($9,318)	($9,578)	($10,374)	($13,552)	($16,762)	($20,289)	($22,855)	($25,143)
Accumulated Other Comprehensive Income	($1,816)	($1,700)	($726)	($179)	($810)	($297)	$1,337	$101	$747	$753
Total Stockholders' Equity	$9,488	$10,281	$11,982	$14,202	$15,146	$15,458	$15,280	$13,383	$14,034	$14,634
Total Liabilities and Stockholders' Equity	$22,534	$23,970	$25,525	$27,838	$29,989	$29,024	$29,392	$28,462	$30,225	$31,975

Source: Morningstar.com.

116

Table 5.12 Walt Disney Company (DIS) Income Statement

USD in Millions Except Per Share Data

Fiscal year ends in September	2001-09	2002-09	2003-09	2004-09	2005-09	2006-09	2007-09	2008-09	2009-09	2010-09	TTM
Revenue	$25,269	$25,329	$27,061	$30,752	$31,944	$34,285	$35,510	$37,843	$36,149	$38,063	$39,537
Cost of Revenue	$21,670	$22,924	$24,330	$26,704	$27,837	$28,807	$28,729	$30,439	$30,452	$31,337	$32,269
Gross Profit	$3,599	$2,405	$2,731	$4,048	$4,107	$5,478	$6,781	$7,404	$5,697	$6,726	$7,268
Operating Expenses											
Restructuring, Merger, and Acquisition	$1,454		$16	$64	$6	($18)					
Other Operating Expenses	$767	$21	$18						$492	$270	$106
Total Operating Expenses	$2,221	$21	$34	$64	$6	($18)					
Operating Income	$1,378	$2,384	$2,697	$3,984	$4,101	$5,496	$6,781	$7,404	$492	$270	$106
Interest Expense	$417	$453	$793	$617	$597	$592	$746	$524	$5,205	$6,456	$7,162
Other Income (Expense)	($841)	$259	$350	$372	$483	$543	$1,690	$522	$466	$456	$402
Income before Taxes	$120	$2,190	$2,254	$3,739	$3,987	$5,447	$7,725	$7,402	$919	$627	$642
Provision for Income Taxes	$1,059	$853	$789	$1,197	$1,241	$1,890	$2,874	$2,673	$5,658	$6,627	$7,402
Other Income	$1,059	($101)	($127)	($197)	($177)	($183)	($177)	($302)	$2,049	$2,314	$2,587
									($302)	($350)	($405)

(Continued)

117

Table 5.12 (Continued)

Fiscal year ends in September	2001-09	2002-09	2003-09	2004-09	2005-09	2006-09	2007-09	2008-09	2009-09	2010-09	TTM
Net Income from Continuing Operations	$120	$1,236	$1,338	$2,345	$2,569	$3,374	$4,674	$4,427	$3,307	$3,963	$4,410
Net Income from Discontinuing Ops							$13				
Cumulative Effect of Accounting Changes	($278)		($71)		($36)						
Net Income	($158)	$1,236	$1,267	$2,345	$2,533	$3,374	$4,687	$4,427	$3,307	$3,963	$4,410
Net Income Available to Common Shareholders	($158)	$1,236	$1,267	$2,345	$2,533	$3,374	$4,687	$4,427	$3,307	$3,963	$4,410
Earnings per Share											
Basic	($0.02)	$0.60	$0.62	$1.14	$1.25	$1.68	$2.34	$2.34	$1.78	$2.07	$2.31
Diluted	($0.02)	$0.61	$0.62	$1.12	$1.22	$1.64	$2.25	$2.28	$1.76	$2.03	$2.27
Weighted Average Shares Outstanding											
Basic	2,085	2,044	2,067	2,049	2,028	2,005	2,004	1,890	1,856	1,915	1,911
Diluted	2,100	2,040	2,043	2,106	2,089	2,076	2,092	1,948	1,875	1,948	1,944

Source: Morningstar.com.

Table 5.13 Walt Disney Company (DIS) Balance Sheet

USD in Millions Except Per Share Data

Fiscal year ends in September	2001-09	2002-09	2003-09	2004-09	2005-09	2006-09	2007-09	2008-09	2009-09	2010-09
Assets										
Current Assets										
Cash										
Cash and Cash Equivalents	$618	$1,239	$1,583	$2,042	$1,723	$2,411	$3,670	$3,001	$3,417	$2,722
Total Cash	$618	$1,239	$1,583	$2,042	$1,723	$2,411	$3,670	$3,001	$3,417	$2,722
Receivables	$3,144	$3,960	$4,018	$4,255	$4,585	$4,707	$5,032	$5,373	$4,854	$5,784
Inventories	$671	$697	$703	$775	$626	$694	$641	$1,124	$1,271	$1,442
Deferred Income Taxes	$622	$624	$674	$772	$749	$592	$862	$1,024	$1,140	$1,018
Prepaid Expenses	$444	$492	$484	$512			$446	$478	$464	$446
Other Current Assets	$1,530	$837	$852	$1,013	$1,162	$1,158	$663	$666	$743	$813
Total Current Assets	$7,029	$7,849	$8,314	$9,369	$8,845	$9,562	$11,314	$11,666	$11,889	$12,225
Non-Current Assets										
Property, Plant, and Equipment										

(Continued)

Table 5.13 (Continued)

Fiscal year ends in September	2001-09	2002-09	2003-09	2004-09	2005-09	2006-09	2007-09	2008-09	2009-09	2010-09
Gross Property, Plant, and Equipment	$20,635	$20,913	$21,472	$28,147	$29,573	$30,948	$32,578	$33,842	$34,992	$36,179
Accumulated Depreciation	($7,728)	($8,133)	($8,794)	($11,665)	($12,605)	($13,781)	($15,145)	($16,310)	($17,395)	($18,373)
Net Property, Plant, and Equipment	$12,907	$12,780	$12,678	$16,482	$16,968	$17,167	$17,433	$17,532	$17,597	$17,806
Equity and Other Investments									$2,554	$2,513
Goodwill						$22,505	$22,085	$22,151	$21,683	$24,100
Intangible Assets	$14,540	$19,859	$19,752	$19,781	$19,705	$8,142	$7,617	$7,822	$2,247	$5,081
Other Long-Term Assets	$9,223	$9,557	$9,244	$8,270	$7,640	$2,622	$2,479	$3,326	$7,147	$7,481
Total Non-Current Assets	$36,670	$42,196	$41,674	$44,533	$44,313	$50,436	$49,614	$50,831	$51,228	$56,981
Total Assets	$43,699	$50,045	$49,988	$53,902	$53,158	$59,998	$60,928	$62,497	$63,117	$69,206
Liabilities and Atockholders' Equity										

Liabilities										
Current Liabilities										
Short-Term Debt	$829	$1,663	$2,457	$4,093	$2,310	$2,682	$3,280	$3,529	$1,206	$2,350
Accounts Payable	$3,822	$3,820	$4,095	$4,531	$5,339	$5,917	$3,996	$4,355	$4,002	$4,413
Accrued Liabilities							$1,953	$1,625	$1,614	$1,484
Deferred Revenues									$2,112	$2,541
Other Current Liabilities	$1,568	$2,336	$2,117	$2,435	$1,519	$1,611	$2,162	$2,082		$212
Total Current Liabilities	$6,219	$7,819	$8,669	$11,059	$9,168	$10,210	$11,391	$11,591	$8,934	$11,000
Non-Current Liabilities										
Long-Term Debt	$8,940	$12,467	$10,643	$9,395	$10,157	$10,843	$11,892	$11,110	$10,130	$11,495
Capital Leases				$339			$274	$226	$224	
Deferred Taxes Liabilities	$2,730	$2,597	$2,712	$2,950	$2,430	$2,651	$2,573	$2,350	$2,630	$1,819
Deferred Revenues								$250	$244	
Pensions and Other Benefits								$3,069	$3,378	

(Continued)

Table 5.13 (Continued)

Fiscal year ends in September	2001-09	2002-09	2003-09	2004-09	2005-09	2006-09	2007-09	2008-09	2009-09	2010-09
Minority Interest	$382	$434	$428	$798	$1,248	$1,343	$1,295	$1,344	$1,691	$1,823
Other Long-term Liabilities	$2,756	$3,283	$3,745	$3,280	$3,945	$3,131	$2,750	$3,779	$1,899	$2,258
Total Non-Current Liabilities	$14,808	$18,781	$17,528	$16,762	$17,780	$17,968	$18,784	$18,583	$20,449	$20,687
Total Liabilities	$21,027	$26,600	$26,197	$27,821	$26,948	$28,178	$30,175	$30,174	$29,383	$31,687
Stockholders' Equity										
Common Stock	$12,096	$12,107	$12,154	$12,447	$13,288	$22,377	$24,207	$26,546	$27,038	$28,736
Retained Earnings	$12,171	$12,979	$13,817	$15,732	$17,775	$20,630	$24,805	$28,413	$31,033	$34,327
Treasury Stock	($1,395)	($1,395)	($1,527)	($1,862)	($4,281)	($11,179)	($18,102)	($22,555)	($22,693)	($23,663)
Accumulated Other Comprehensive Income	($200)	($246)	($653)	($236)	($572)	($8)	($157)	($81)	($1,644)	($1,881)
Total Stockholders' Equity	$22,672	$23,445	$23,791	$26,081	$26,210	$31,820	$30,753	$32,323	$33,734	$37,519
Total Liabilities and Stockholders' Equity	$43,699	$50,045	$49,988	$53,902	$53,158	$59,998	$60,928	$62,497	$63,117	$69,206

Source: Morningstar.com.

Table 5.14 Ford Motor Co (F) Income Statement

USD in Millions Except Per Share Data

Fiscal year ends in December	2001-12	2002-12	2003-12	2004-12	2005-12	2006-12	2007-12	2008-12	2009-12	2010-12	TTM
Revenue	$162,412	$163,420	$164,196	$171,652	$177,089	$160,123	$172,455	$146,277	$118,308	$128,954	$130,502
Cost of Revenue	$134,892	$125,137	$129,821	$135,856	$144,944	$148,869	$143,255	$128,977	$100,016	$104,451	$106,088
Gross Profit	$27,520	$38,283	$34,375	$35,796	$32,145	$11,254	$29,200	$17,300	$18,292	$24,503	$24,414
Operating Expenses											
Sales, General, and Administrative	$13,602	$28,426	$17,480	$25,115	$24,652	$19,180	$21,169	$21,430	$13,258	$11,909	$11,554
Other Operating Expenses	$21,486		$8,779						$7,858	$5,936	$5,396
Total Operating Expenses	$35,088	$28,426	$26,259	$25,115	$24,652	$19,180	$21,169	$21,430	$21,116	$17,845	$16,950
Operating Income	($7,568)	$9,857	$8,116	$10,681	$7,493	($7,926)	$8,031	($4,130)	($2,824)	$6,658	$7,464
Interest Expense	$10,848	$8,824	$7,690	$7,071	$7,643	$8,783	$10,927	$10,437	$7,858	$6,368	$5,828
Other Income (Expense)	$10,832	($80)	$944	$1,243	$2,146	$1,658	($850)	$163	$13,708	$6,859	$6,154

(Continued)

Table 5.14 (Continued)

Fiscal year ends in December	2001-12	2002-12	2003-12	2004-12	2005-12	2006-12	2007-12	2008-12	2009-12	2010-12	TTM
Income before Taxes	($7,584)	$953	$1,370	$4,853	$1,996	($15,051)	($3,746)	($14,404)	$3,026	$7,149	$7,790
Provision for Income Taxes	($2,151)	$302	$135	$937	($512)	($2,646)	($1,294)	$63	$69	$592	$762
Other Income	($20)	($367)	($314)	($282)	($280)	($210)	($312)	($214)			
Net Income from Continuing Operations	($5,453)	$284	$921	$3,634	$2,228	($12,615)	($2,764)	($14,681)	$2,957	$6,557	$7,028
Net Income from Discontinuing Ops		($262)	($162)	($147)	$47	$2	$41	$9	$5		
Cumulative Effect of Accounting Changes		($1,002)	($264)		($251)						
Other									($245)	$4	($1)
Net Income	($5,453)	($980)	$495	$3,487	$2,024	($12,613)	($2,723)	($14,672)	$2,717	$6,561	$7,027

Preferred Dividend	$15	$15	$152								
Net Income Available to Common Shareholders	($5,468)	($995)	$495	$3,335	$2,024	($12,613)	($2,723)	($14,672)	$2,717	$6,561	$7,027
Earnings per Share											
Basic	($3.02)	($0.55)	$0.27	$1.91	$1.10	($6.72)	($1.38)	($6.46)	$0.91	$1.90	$1.98
Diluted	($3.02)	($0.54)	$0.27	$1.73	$1.05	($6.72)	($1.38)	($6.46)	$0.86	$1.66	$1.71
Weighted Average Shares Outstanding											
Basic	1,820	1,819	1,832	1,830	1,846	1,879	1,979	2,273	2,992	3,449	3,550
Diluted	1,820	1,819	1,832	1,830	1,846	1,879	1,979	2,273	2,992	4,178	4,102

Source: Morningstar.com.

Table 5.15 Ford Motor Co (F) Balance Sheet

USD in Millions Except Per Share Data

Fiscal year ends in December	2001-12	2002-12	2003-12	2004-12	2005-12	2006-12	2007-12	2008-12	2009-12	2010-12
Assets										
Current Assets										
Cash										
Cash and Cash Equivalents	$7,218	$12,250	$21,770	$23,511	$31,499	$28,894	$35,283	$22,049	$21,441	$14,805
Short-Term Investments	$10,949	$18,271	$17,539	$10,565	$11,044	$26,728	$15,515	$17,411	$38,657	$32,440
Total Cash	$18,167	$30,521	$39,309	$34,076	$42,543	$55,622	$50,798	$39,460	$60,098	$47,245
Receivables	$2,214	$2,065	$2,721	$5,971	$114,497	$106,863	$109,053	$93,484	$84,583	$77,458
Inventories	$6,191	$6,980	$9,181	$10,766	$10,271	$11,578	$10,121	$8,618	$5,450	$5,917
Deferred Income Taxes	$2,595		$3,225	$4,830	$5,881					
Other Current Assets	$7,093	$154,703	$117,732	$154,513	$26,950	$8,772	$8,210	$6,073		
Total Current Assets	$36,260	$194,269	$172,168	$210,156	$200,142	$182,835	$178,182	$147,635	$150,131	$130,620
Non-Current Assets										
Property, Plant, and Equipment										

Gross Property, Plant, and Equipment	$60,631	$62,935	$72,105	$75,564	$73,324	$77,023	$72,800	$66,802	$60,182	$57,079
Accumulated Depreciation	($27,510)	($25,000)	($30,112)	($31,013)	($32,617)	($38,518)	($36,561)	($38,237)	($35,404)	($33,900)
Net Property, Plant, and Equipment	$33,121	$37,935	$41,993	$44,551	$40,707	$38,505	$36,239	$28,565	$24,778	$23,179
Equity and Other Investments						$5,839	$2,069	$1,593	$1,550	$2,569
Goodwill						$1,098			$209	$102
Intangible Assets	$5,996	$6,617	$7,262	$7,271	$5,945					
Deferred Income Taxes		$15,213	$12,092			$4,950	$3,500	$3,108	$3,440	$2,003
Other Long-Term Assets	$201,166	$35,323	$82,405	$30,676	$22,682	$45,327	$59,274	$37,427	$14,742	$6,214
Total Non-Current Assets	$240,283	$95,088	$143,752	$82,498	$69,334	$95,719	$101,082	$70,693	$44,719	$34,067
Total Assets	$276,543	$289,357	$315,920	$292,654	$269,476	$278,554	$279,264	$218,328	$194,850	$164,687
Liabilities and Stockholders' Equity										

(Continued)

Table 5.15 (Continued)

Fiscal year ends in December	2001-12	2002-12	2003-12	2004-12	2005-12	2006-12	2007-12	2008-12	2009-12	2010-12
Liabilities										
Current Liabilities										
Short-Term Debt	$302		$29,573			$27,676	$28,275	$63,662		
Accounts Payable	$15,677	$18,981	$20,420	$21,489	$22,813	$23,549	$20,832	$14,772		
Accrued Liabilities	$23,990	$25,088	$32,171	$31,187	$72,977	$24,287	$23,579	$28,728	$46,599	$43,844
Deferred Revenues						$4,708	$4,093	$3,667		
Other Current Liabilities	$4,577	$56,276	$124						$14,594	$16,362
Total Current Liabilities	$44,546	$100,345	$82,288	$52,676	$95,790	$80,220	$76,779	$110,829	$61,193	$60,206
Non-Current Liabilities										
Long-Term Debt	$167,035	$162,222	$150,231	$172,973	$154,332	$144,373	$140,255	$90,534	$132,441	$103,988
Deferred Taxes Liabilities	$10,065	$14,561	$13,413	$6,171	$5,275	$2,744	$3,034	$2,035	$2,375	$1,135
Minority Interest	$672	$5,670	$659	$877	$1,122	$1,159	$1,421	$1,195	$1,305	$31

Other Long-Term Liabilities	$46,439	$969	$57,678	$43,912	$53,523	$52,147	$31,046	$5,356		
Total Non-Current Liabilities	$224,211	$183,422	$221,981	$223,933	$160,729	$201,799	$196,857	$124,810	$141,477	$105,154
Total Liabilities	$268,757	$283,767	$304,269	$276,609	$256,519	$282,019	$273,636	$235,639	$202,670	$165,360
Stockholders' Equity										
Common Stock	$19	$19	$19	$19	$19	$19	$22	$24	$34	$38
Additional Paid-In Capital	$6,001	$5,420	$5,374	$5,321	$4,872	$4,562	$7,834	$9,076	$16,786	$20,803
Retained Earnings	$10,502	$8,659	$8,421	$11,175	$12,461	($17)	($1,485)	($16,145)	($13,599)	($7,038)
Treasury Stock	($2,823)	($1,977)	($1,749)	($1,728)	($833)	($183)	($185)	($181)	($177)	($163)
Accumulated Other Comprehensive Income	($5,913)	($6,531)	($414)	$1,258	($3,562)	($7,846)	($558)	($10,085)	($10,864)	($14,313)
Total Stockholders' Equity	$7,786	$5,590	$11,651	$16,045	$12,957	($3,465)	$5,628	($17,311)	($7,820)	($673)
Total Liabilities and Stockholders' Equity	$276,543	$289,357	$315,920	$292,654	$269,476	$278,554	$279,264	$218,328	$194,850	$164,687

Source: Morningstar.com.

Figure 5.2   Building a Small Business Warren Buffett Would Love the Flowchart

CHAPTER 6

The Tumor of Long-Term Debt

Debt: Friend or Foe?

When it comes to the subject of debt, there seem to be two opposing thoughts in the world of financial gurus.

Either:

1. Debt is good and should be used in large quantities to leverage business and real estate investments.

Or:

2. The presence of any level of debt on the balance sheet, even for business and investment purposes, is the equivalent to standing next to the gates of hell.

So, which is correct? Is debt a good thing that can lead to riches or is it a fast track to eternal damnation? Let us turn to our coach, Warren Buffett, for the answer.

First, though, let us evaluate the two debt paradigms in the eyes of the paradigmers.

Wrapping Your Brain around Debt versus No Debt

1. *Debt is good and should be used in large quantities to leverage business and real estate investments.*

Two primary reasons exist for the advocacy of investment debt:

1. The use of other people's money, or OPM
2. The benefits of leverage

As an investor/business owner, it is not necessary to start your own business using your own personal cache of money if you can use other people's money, which in most cases is the bank's money. The bank, of course, does not freely hand out money (there's this thing called interest), and they want to see that you can repay the loan via the cash flow of the business. Typically, this proof of the pudding is found in the business's cash flow projection. The bank knows that in many cases the projection is merely a forecasted best guess, and they prefer that other sources of income, such as a spouse's paycheck, are available in case the business heads south of the border quickly.

The Second, but Certainly Not the Least, Important Factor—Leverage

If you put $20,000 down on a $100,000 rental property and it generates $3,000 a year in cash flow, what is your rate of return?

Answer: $3,000/$20,000 or 15 percent

If the property increases in value by 6 percent, how much have you gained?

Answer: $100,000 × 6% = $6,000

In this case, what is your return on investment?

Answer: $6,000/$20,000 = 30%

When you add this to your $3,000 a month of cash flow, what is your true rate of return?

Answer:

Rental Cash Flow: $3,000

+ Appreciation: $6,000

Total = $9,000

$9,000/$20,000 or 45%

You can also simply add the two rates of return to find the 45 percent return: 30% + 15% = 45%.

If instead you took that money and invested it in a stock market mutual fund, how much rate of return would you expect? Answer: 10 percent maybe, over the long haul.

Stocks: 10%

Real Estate: 45%

A major principle of leverage is that you are doing more with less and creating the potential for a high return on equity and return on investment. If instead of $20,000, the investor puts down the full $100,000, the return on equity in the property will be 9 percent, ($9,000/$100,000) versus 45 percent. Of course, the individual in scenario one is saddled with $80,000 worth of debt. So why is this so bad?

2. *The presence of any level of debt on the balance sheet, even for business and investment purposes, is the equivalent to standing next to the gates of hell.*

Two reasons to hate debt:

1. The reverse effects of leverage
2. The confusion between good debt and bad debt

This Is a Two-Way Street—The Reverse Effects of Leverage

Just as leverage can magnify returns as values increase, it can also magnify losses as values drop. In our cash-flowing rental property example, let us pretend that instead of increasing in value, the property decreases in value by 10 percent. Real estate is typically seen as a steady, non-volatile asset class (unlike the stock market), which over the long term consistently increases in value by 4 to 6 percent a year, but there are occasions (think 2007 to 2008) when real estate values drop.

Instead of increasing in value by 6 percent, let us analyze our investment factoring in a 10 percent *drop* in value.

If the property drops in value by 10 percent, how much have you lost?

Answer: $100,000 × 10% = −$10,000

Based on the initial investment of $20,000, what is the percentage loss?

Answer: $10,000/$20,000 = 50%

In the world of stocks, however, a 10 percent loss would only equate to a $2,000 loss (10% × $20,000).

Additionally, if your rental property asset has dropped in value, it is safe to assume that not all is well with the economy and rents might also suffer. Let us assume that rents drop from $3,000 to $2,000 in the rental scenario. The total return during the downturn will be −40% (−$8,000/$20,000).

Most real estate investors only pay attention to the cash flow. In the long haul, is it safe to say that real estate will continue to increase in value? I believe the answer is yes, it will. As long as inflation exists, real estate values should generally increase. In the real estate world, economic downturns are truly detrimental when cash flow turns negative and the investor is unable to pay the bills. As long as the up-front cash flow analysis is detailed and accurate; the financing terms are favorable; and quality property management, that does not let the property depreciate into a trash heap, is in place, the risk should be mitigated.

My Poor, Poor Income Statement—Damn You, Debt!

Debt becomes a huge anchor weight when an investment or business can no longer use cash flow to make the debt payment. For example, in the rental property scenario, if the cash flow is slim as a result of large debt service due to a large amount of debt, what happens if the rental market tanks? See Table 6.1.

Table 6.1   Economic Downturn Impact on a Debt-laden Income Statement

	This . . .	Becomes This . . .
Monthly CF Analysis		
Monthly Gross Rental Income	$1,275	$1,000
Minus Vacancy Loss of 8%	$102	$80
Total Income	$1,173	$920
Monthly Expenses		
Property Management Fee of 10%	$117	$92
Accounting	$10	$10
Insurance (Hazard)	$50	$50
Yard Work	$15	$15
Repairs and Maintenance	$90	$90
Miscellaneous	$10	$10
Reserves	$20	$20
Taxes (Property)	$100	$100
Total Expenses	$412	$387
NOI	$761	$533
Loan Payment	$700	$700
Cash Flow	$61	($167)
Total Cash Put into Property	$20,750	$20,750
Cash on Cash Return	$0	($0)

You can see that before the downturn, the cash flow of the property is $61 a month, an annualized 4 percent return on the initial investment, providing a tiny amount of wiggle room. When rents decrease, the cash flow turns negative, the property starts losing $167 a month, and the property owner may now have trouble paying the bills.

The same income statement scenario applies to small businesses as well. If the cash flow margin is slim at best, then the slightest souring of the economy can send the cash flow and earnings into negative territory.

Good Debt Versus Bad Debt

Another reason why excessive debt can lead to bad results is that many people confuse the definitions of good debt and bad debt. Once the line becomes blurred, individuals load up the balance sheet with both good debt and bad debt, claiming that it is all good and justifying the purchase of toys.

Some Clarification

As a rule of thumb, good debt is any debt used to buy assets that generally appreciate in value and deliver cash flow each month into your income statement. Bad debt is debt used to purchase wasting assets that potentially require dollars for maintenance and upkeep (jet skis, plasma TVs, boats, cars, lawn tractors with roll bars). More specifically, Robert Kiyosaki, author of *Rich Dad, Poor Dad*, states that good debt is used to purchase assets that put money in your pocket, such as rental property, dividend paying stocks, and franchise businesses, and that bad debt is used to purchase toys or "doodads" that take money out of your pocket each month—jet skis, plasma TVs, cars, and so on.

He even goes so far as to say that a mortgage on your personal residence is bad debt since, although the house is appreciating in value, the house is taking money out of your pocket on a monthly basis through upkeep and maintenance, taxes, and insurance.

This last definition, in my opinion, is an extremely conservative definition of bad debt. A mortgage on a house in my opinion is relatively neutral and neither good debt nor bad debt. Although a personal residence creates monthly expenses, the house value is appreciating, making it a wash on the monthly expenses; and it is not financially prudent to rent over a lifetime. An individual who rents for 50 years from the age of 25, paying an average monthly rent of $700, will end up paying $420,000 over a lifetime. If the rents increase at 4 percent a year, the renter will end up paying well over one million dollars in rent—$1,282,409, to be exact.

I don't know about you but I can find "bearable" accommodations for half a million dollars.

Bad debt examples:

- Automobiles
- Credit cards
- TVs
- School loans

Good debt examples:

- Rental property
- Businesses

Neutral debt:

- Home mortgages

Warren Buffett versus Good Debt versus Bad Debt versus Your Small Business—Who Wins?

So, which argument is correct? Is it true that having any amount of debt is the equivalent to standing outside the gates of hell, or is the investor who is bereft of debt losing out on the leverage advantages of debt?

Let us turn to referee Warren Buffett for a ruling and see how it applies to a small business.

Warren Speaks!

Warren likes companies that have the ability to pay off their long-term debt in one to two years straight out of earnings.[1] In other words, he likes businesses with one to two times earnings of long-term debt on the balance sheet and no more. If I have a business that earns $10,000 a year, then ideally, in order to make Warren Buffett happy (or to help him fall in love), the balance sheet will have no more than $20,000 in long-term debt. This is a fairly high standard, but in the world of Warren Buffett this is another indicator of a great business that is spewing off tons of cash and has no need for huge amounts of debt. Additionally, if times get tight as in our rental property's income statement example, the business will have plenty of wiggle room to pay the bills and potentially still have earnings.

Peter Speaks!

One of Warren Buffett's contemporaries, Peter Lynch, formerly of the Magellan Fund and author of *One Up on Wall Street*, likes companies that have a debt to equity ratio of 33 percent or less.[2] This means that for every one dollar in debt, a company should have $3.03 in equity. To use the financing of a car as an analogy, if I own a car worth $10,000, then ideally I would have no more than $2,500 in debt. Of course, car debt is considered bad debt, so even this amount of debt doesn't make sense in context. If I own a business asset worth $100,000, the debt on the balance sheet should be no more than $25,000 under the Peter Lynch paradigm, and if the debt is mostly long-term debt, then the net earnings on the income statement should be at least $8,333 under the Warren Buffett paradigm. (The company should have the ability to retire long-term debt strictly from earnings in one to two years.)

Thus, Warren Buffett is neither completely of the view that having business debt is the equivalent to standing next to the gates of hell, nor does he believe in using excessive debt for leverage. If anything, he leans toward the side of little to no debt (companies with snowballing debt and interest payments will eventually run out of room for earnings, leading to a petering out of return on equity), and he would argue that bad personal debt for toys such as jet skis and plasma TVs is bad debt, pure and simple, since it draws away from investment capital.

Crossing the Streams

When it comes to debt, both the leverage community and the standing next to the gates of hell community agree that personal debt is bad. In the leverage paradigm, personal debt does not put money in your pocket on a monthly basis (no cash flow), and in the fire and brimstone community, debt detracts from investment capital and creates risk. Bad debt removes cash from your wallet each month and typically is used to finance the purchase of wasting assets. In addition, excessive debt leaves little wiggle room in the financial statements and can lead to bad results in the event of an economic downturn.

So, the debt prescription is as follows:

- Zero personal debt.
- Conservative amounts of business and investment debt in order to purchase cash flowing assets.
- No more than one to three years of earnings in long-term debt in a business or investment.
- Maintain a conservative debt to equity ratio of 33 percent or less.

How to Wire the Debt Prescription into a Small Business

The first step in applying the debt formula to your small business is to pull out ye olde balance sheet and income statement for the last complete fiscal year. In other words, grab last year's tax returns.

1. On the balance sheet, find the item labeled "total non-current assets" and the corresponding dollar figure. This is the business's long-term debt. Write it down.
2. Next, find the net earnings or net income figure on the income statement. Write it down.
3. Divide the total long-term debt from step one by last year's earnings found in step two.
4. What is the result?

If the resulting number is less than or equal to two, then congratulations, you are conservatively financed and should continue to maintain or reduce this level of debt. If the result is greater than two, then you are above the Warren Buffett debt level definition of a conservatively financed strong business, and it may be wise to formulate and implement a debt reduction plan. If the resultant number is many times the magical number of two, say twice as much or five times as much, then it may be time to think about amputating some nonproducing assets by selling them and using the proceeds to pay down the debt.

Peter Lynch Has a Say as Well . . . What Say You, Peter Lynch?

To apply the Peter Lynch check, you simply take the total debt from the balance sheet and divide it by the total equity, again from the balance sheet. (Remember, assets minus liabilities equals equity.) Anything less than or equal to 33 percent is good according to Peter Lynch.

But What If I Am Starting a Business?

If the business is a start-up, then truly, once again, it all comes back down to the reliability and accuracy of the financial projections. Chiefly, the two main nuts within this soup will be the projected earnings and the long-term debt load needed to start the business.

In many ways, it might be prudent to take the yearly earnings from the end of, say, year three, since the first two years will be a part of the start-up curve and it will take some time to ramp up earnings to the "norm." Keep in mind, though, that these are just projections, but perhaps accurate ones that you produced with a reality-tempered mindset.

The Same Methodology Applies to the Start-Up Business

- Determine the long-term debt balance. If the initial debt balance will be abnormally high due to start-up financing, then, as in the case of earnings, use the year three, end-of-year balance sheet.
- Divide the long-term debt by the total earnings.

If the result is three or less, then in terms of debt it appears that this start-up weighs out pretty good on the Warren Buffett debt scale. Again, though, with a start-up it all comes back down to how reliable the forecasts are—garbage in, garbage out.

If the number is much greater than three, say a 10, then you may want to consider different financing options, such as saving a larger down payment, or if the business is not meeting the other Buffett criteria in addition to the debt criteria, you may want to look elsewhere.

Stocks Versus Real Estate Investing

Time and again the battle royal over stocks versus real estate investing simmers to rapid boil and it is high time to throw down the gauntlet and examine the arguments in order to gain better perspective on building a small business that Warren Buffett would love. Remember, three major investment asset classes exist, and we have already covered a handful of intersections, from Warren Buffet's business-like stock investments, to rental property as a business, to Hawaiian-themed, tomato-sauce spewing pizzerias. It is very important to understand why folks dig in and defend their positions in order to truly develop a personal expertise instead of lining up like a dull lemming.

The proponents of leverage argue that real estate has many advantages over stock investing. But as a small business owner turned Warren Buffett business perspective small business owner, you aren't going to necessarily invest like Joe Consumer. If you invest in either rental property or stocks from a business perspective, the advantages of real estate over stocks will not necessarily apply. Still, just for a second, let us put on the glasses of a real estate leverage advocate. Here are the advantages according to a property proponent.

The Advantages of Real Estate

Cash Flow   The chief thing regarding cash flow is that the property is self-maintaining as far as expenses go. [3] It is a business model in itself—the income minus the outflow equals the cash flow. All expenses should first be covered in order for the investment to make sense, and second, the property should generate cash flow, which adds icing to the cake of property appreciation. When comparing real estate investing to stock investing, it is important to compare not only the national average real estate appreciation rate of 6 percent to the historic average stock market return of 10 percent; you must also factor in the cash flow received.

In addition, the cash flow is passive. Although you might have to handle tenant issues, arrange for repairs, or do them yourself, your physical presence is not required all the time in order to generate the income. In the stock universe, cash flow must be generated via dividends unless you plan on dipping into capital gains or principal. Although it is not impossible to generate a healthy amount of cash flow through dividends, it is difficult to find yields that match the 10 to 15 percent rates of return on money invested in rental property. In addition, dividend stocks must be monitored for dividend cuts and omissions, just as rental property must be managed for vacancy and repairs and maintenance.

Once passive cash flow from investments is equal to or greater than expenses, an individual is financially independent.

Control   In the stock universe the individual stock investor does not have much control over a business's operations or management—unless, of course, you are Warren Buffet and own a controlling interest (or the entire company). Thus, it is really difficult for an individual investor to have an impact on the company's financial results. Sure, you get a proxy vote, but unless you own a large percentage of shares, this won't amount to much. If you own shares of Coca Cola, you can buy up all of the Coke at your local supermarket warehouse in order to ratchet up sales, but considering they had $35 billion in sales last year, this effort would pop, fizz, and fail.

In the real estate universe, if you own a rental property, you can increase rents, screen tenants, throw in some new landscaping, paint the walls, drive by the property in the evenings and check its appearance. If rents drop in the area by $25, you can drop your rent rates and keep vacancy rates low. If prices go up, you can raise rents. In real estate you have much more control over the investment, unless you use property management. In stocks, the control comes through the initial and follow-up analysis in order to make wise buy, sell, and hold decisions.

A Side Note on Hypocrisy   Within the land of rental property aficionados, there exists a blazing hypocrisy. An owner who manages a rental property in order to gain control has lost the passivity of the investment. On the other hand, a property owner who enlists the services of property management has lost the control. The investment has now turned passive—just like a mutual fund. Touché!

Appreciation   Real estate on average appreciates 6 percent nationally. Although this has not been the case recently, let us use a long-term lens in order to compare the two asset behemoths. Stocks appreciate on average at 10 percent over the long term, real estate at 6 percent. The problem with the simple 10 percent versus 6 percent rate comparison, from a property investor's point of view, is that it does not take leverage into account.

Leverage   If you put $20,000 down on a $100,000 property and it generates $3,000 a year in cash flow, what is your rate of return? It is $3,000/$20,000 or 15 percent.

If the property increases in value by 6 percent, how much have you gained?

Answer: $100,000 × 6% = $6,000

How much of a rate of return is this over your initial investment?

Answer: $6,000/$20,000 = 30%

When you add this to your $3,000 of cash flow, your true rate of return is $9,000/$20,000 or 45 percent.

If instead, you took the money and invested it in a stock mutual fund, how much rate of return can you expect?

Answer: 10 percent over the long haul.

Stocks: 10 percent

Real Estate: 45 percent

'Nuff said.

Additionally, one of the pros of a rental real estate investment is that the tenant is paying down the mortgage and buying the asset for the investor over time. Thank you, Mr. Tenant!

Refinance   If you increase the property value you can refinance it and withdraw the money tax-free. Say you finance a $200,000 property and, through a property improvement plan (reduction in vacancy rates due to detailed tenant screening, rental increases based on rent premiums for ground floor apartments, bidding out the landscaping at a cheaper rate), the property is now worth $250,000. It will now be possible to refinance the property for $250,000, pay off the initial $200,000, and withdraw the $50,000 tax-free. (Of course you now owe the bank $250,000, and cash flow may be a touch tighter.)

Depreciation   This is one of those lovely phantom tax deductions a property investor gets to claim at the end of the year, and it will turn rental money into 0 percent tax money. According to *Rich Dad's* Robert Kiyosaki, your earned income is taxed at 50 percent, your portfolio income or dividend income is taxed at 15 percent, and your passive or rental income can be taxed at 0%.

Here's how:

You get to depreciate residential real estate property over 27.5 years and commercial over 39 years. If a property produces cash flows at $20,000 a year with depreciation of $25,000, then it generates a tax loss of $5,000 and no tax is paid on income. It can be argued that the property is depreciating and generating a real repair cost, but this expense is already accounted for in the income statement and major disaster repairs should be covered by insurance.

The depreciation equation:

$$\text{(Total Asset Value} - \text{Land Value)/Depreciable Years}$$
$$= \text{Annual Depreciation}$$

Asset Protection   Two things here: insurance and incorporation. If a stock drops 50 percent in value, what protection do you have? Perhaps a stop loss order or a put option. If a rental property investment burns down, what protection do you have?

Answer: Insurance

The second form of protection is incorporation. By placing your property in the bucket of a legal entity, you shield off your personal assets from most legal attacks stemming from the property.

Question: Why do you drive on a parkway and park in a driveway?

Answer: Who knows.

1031 Exchanges   A property investor can roll over property gains tax-free by buying bigger properties using a 1031 Exchange. The capital gains do not go away—they carry forward, but by using a 1031 exchange, you can continue to roll those gains into bigger and maybe better properties tax-free. If you finish out the game and choose not to hold the last property or roll it, you will have tax consequences.

Hedge Against Inflation   Because real estate is a tangible asset, it will generally rise at the rate of inflation or higher. Historically inflation has averaged 4.1 percent a year. This means real estate, with its average historical appreciation of 6 percent, has beaten inflation by nearly 2 percent, not taking into account cash flow.

A Physical Asset   As a property owner, you can walk up to a piece of rental property, touch it, taste it, feel it. You can inspect it, visit the tenants, see the cracks forming in the walls, observe the beer cans and old tires accumulating in the front yard. With a stock, in many respects, it is a piece of intangible equity that exists in the ether. Sure, if you own Coke you can drink Coke and you can go visit Coke headquarters in Atlanta. If you own McDonald's you can slip through the drive thru, order some nuggets, Filet o' Fish, and say hello to Grimace, Officer Big Mac, and Mayor McCheese. But the investment in this case truly lives throughout the intricate business system composed of hundreds of bottlers and Mc-franchises. A property, on the other hand, has the attribute of direct management potential. (Unless, of course, you farm this job out to property management.)

In Conclusion

Real estate investing has many perceived advantages over stock investing (just as owning equity in companies with 120 years of brand building and billions of dollars in revenues a year has many advantages over owning a duplex with an Impala in the front yard and a Schlitz guzzling tenant named Phil), and many analysts neglect to make a fair comparison between the two. Many merely compare the 6 percent appreciation in real estate to the 10 percent return in stocks. What is mainly being left out are the benefits of passive cash flow, leverage, and depreciation. Once these three factors are included in the mix, it is clear that real estate has some unique advantages over stocks.

As if it is not glaringly apparent, I like real estate investments, but I do not wholeheartedly pony up to the "real estate as the greatest thing since sex" mantra. There is something to be said about owning equity in companies that deal in mouse ears, macaroni, and McRibs, and I believe in investing across the investment spectrum of stocks, real estate, and business in order to diversify. Diversification to me is more than just owning a handful of mutual funds.

In order to build a small business that Warren Buffett would love, it is very important to understand why people love what they say they love, whether it is real estate or equity in the big companies. You must develop your own personal business acumen, which will make you a stealthy ninja in building a business that Warren Buffett would love. Figure 6.1 continues the road map we've been following.

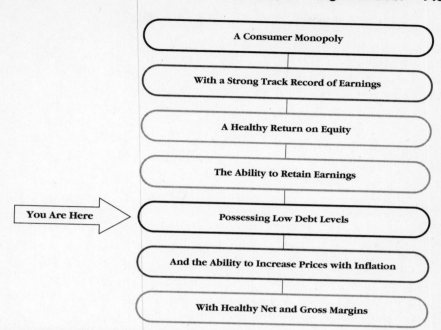

Figure 6.1   Building a Small Business Warren Buffett Would Love Flowchart

CHAPTER 7

Keeping Up with the Joneses

In building a business that Warren Buffett would love it is imperative to build one that has the ability to increase prices with inflation and pay off fixed debt with cheaper dollars. Why? A business that can keep up with inflation while maintaining or buying back shares will increase its earnings per share; a business with 1 million shares outstanding and $1 million in earnings will increase its earnings per share from $1 to $1.40 if earnings increase to $1.4 million due to an increase in prices as a result of keeping up with inflation.

This is the opposite of businesses that are price competitive and must maintain a competitive edge through flat and/or gutted out, discounted pricing (think automotive, steel, aluminum).

Hamburgers, Cokes, and Animated Mice . . . Oh My!

Let us examine the pricing inflation of three token consumer monopolies, businesses that at one time or another Warren Buffet has been in love with: McDonald's, Coke, and Disney. See Table 7.1.

In 1955 a McDonald's hamburger cost 15 cents. In 2011 the same flapjack of greasy goodness cost 95 cents. A Coke in 1950 cost a nickel and in 2011 the same bottle of liquid sweetness (sans the cocaine) cost approximately $1.00, depending on location. Believe it or not, a ticket to Disney World cost $3.50 in 1971 and $80 in 2010.[1] At one point in history you could have gone to Disney World, had lunch, and drunk a tasty bottle of sugar water, all for about

Table 7.1   Price Inflation

Price of a McDonald's Hamburger		Price of a Coke		Price of a Ticket to Disney World	
1955	$0.15	1950	$0.05	1971	$3.50
2011	$0.95	2011	$1.00	2010	$80.00

$3.70. Good golly! Nowadays, the total for this Disney day out comes to about $81.95. The hamburger has increased in price by 533 percent, the Coke by 1,900 percent, and the Disney ticket by a whopping 2,186 percent! Now that is inflation, folks, and guess what? In each case, the company stands to benefit, even though its own costs are rising.

Just What Is Inflation?

In general terms, inflation can be defined as the U.S. dollar buying less and less over time. It is a sustained increase in the general level of prices for goods and services, and in many ways, as far as the consumer is concerned, it provides good fodder for bitching about the prices of groceries, but it also creates the perception of wealth: Salaries increase and housing values increase. Joe Consumer becomes a made-man once his house value increases from $100,000 to $125,000. The catch, though, is that his expenses have also gone up.

Also, as the government prints more and more money, more dollars end up in circulation, all of them competing for the same goods. As more dollars compete for these goods, prices go up.

Thus, the reason why it takes a dollar today to buy a Coke that cost a nickel in 1950 (which in my opinion had more of a value add kick) is that more dollars are competing for the same bottle. Twenty years ago the average worker could buy a box of Kellogg's cereal using half an hour's worth of wages. Today the same is true: The average worker can work half an hour and buy a box of cereal. How 'bout them apples?

So What? How Does This Apply to My Small Business?

Okay, so a McDonald's hamburger, a bottle of Coke, and a ticket to Disney World have all dramatically increased in price over the years, and the companies each stood to benefit even with rising costs on their income statements. How is this so and how does it apply to a small business?

This is how:

A company with the ability to increase prices along with inflation benefits when the number of its shares outstanding stays the same or some shares are bought back. Again, a business with 1 million shares outstanding and $1 million in earnings will increase its earnings per share from $1 to $1.40 if earnings increase to $1.4 million as a result of price increases. The business also stands to benefit if the balance sheet has an element of long-term fixed debt. In the first scenario, as prices increase the company raises prices on its products, whether hamburgers, Cokes, or mouse-ear tickets, thus increasing revenues on the income statement.

Let's say I own a chocolate bar company, let us call it Schmershey's, and let's pretend that I sell chocolate bars for a dollar. As a result of inflation, I raise the price of my chocolate bars to $1.25. This is great, but also keep in mind that the expenses on my income statement are inflating as well. Let's say that for every dollar I make in the chocolate bar business, 30 cents makes it to the bottom line. So, when I was charging a buck for bar of chocolate, 30 cents made it to earnings. Now that I am charging $1.25, 38 cents is finding its way to the earnings bucket. Ah-ha! With inflation, even though the expense items in my income statement increased, I was able to raise prices and deliver more to the bottom line. See Table 7.2.

You can see in our simple example that, with the increase in prices due to inflation and the subsequent inflating of the bottom line, earnings per share increase from $.15 to $.19. If you and I are the only shareholders, inflation just effectively increased our earnings per share by 27 percent. Keep in mind, though, that this math

Table 7.2   Impact of Price Inflation on the Income Statement

	This	Becomes This . . .
Gross Income	$1.00	$1.25
Net Income	$0.30	$0.38
Shares Outstanding	2	2
Earnings per Share	$0.15	$0.19

Table 7.3   Stagnant Prices versus Inflation

	This	Becomes This . . .
Gross Income	$1.00	$1.00
Net Income	$0.30	$0.20
Shares Outstanding	2	2
Earnings per Share	$0.15	$0.10

is dependent on the number of shares outstanding remaining the same or, even better, decreasing through buybacks.

The Opposite Is Also True

The company that can index its prices to inflation has an evil twin that should be avoided in building a small business that Warren Buffett would love. This evil twin company is the one that can't raise prices along with inflation (again, think automotive, aluminum, steel). In these types of businesses, earnings per share remain the same or potentially decrease, since price competition is so stiff (can't raise prices) and costs are inflating (expenses on the income statement are increasing). See Table 7.3.

Price competitive industries contain companies that must fight it out with their competitors and tend to eke out a slim profit. Essentially, they tear each other apart. In these types of businesses, the customer does not care what brand name you slap on the product, as long as it is up to quality and is price competitive. If another company offers the product at the same or better quality at a cheaper price, the customer will simply jump ship. I guarantee that if you are idling at your local gas station and the pump across the street lowers its prices by $.25 right in front of your eyes, you will merrily hop across the street to snag the cheaper fuel. Alas, in these businesses it is highly important to keep prices competitive and not necessarily to keep up with inflation.

An Either-Or World

If the world was comprised of businesses that fit exclusively into either-or buckets regarding inflation (either they can all raise prices or none of them can), then our business and investment decisions would not care one nickel about inflation. We would invest and build businesses regardless of the effects, since everyone is in the same boat: Everyone is either price competitive or price-ratcheting. But since the world is composed of two distinct beasts as it relates to inflation, those that can raise prices with inflation and those that cannot, it is very important to pay strict attention in order to build a business that Warren Buffett would love. To earn his love you must build a business that can raise prices with inflation.

Again, since everything is relative (revenues increase, expenses increase), the inflation feature is beneficial as it relates to potentially static features of the income statement and balance sheet: number of shares outstanding and long-term fixed debt. In the second scenario, revenues increase and expenses increase, but fixed interest payments remain the same.

Fixed Debt Can Be Your Friend—Hello, Friend

Small businesses typically benefit in the fixed debt scenario. As prices inflate, revenues increase, the fixed debt remains fixed, and the business is able to pay off the long-term debt with inflated dollars. In other words, the business is receiving more bucks (along with larger expenses, which also inflate), but the debt payment remains the same. See Table 7.4.

This phenomenon, if you can call it that, has been coined as "letting the bank buy your asset for you," since the bank is locked in at a fixed interest rate and you are paying off the debt with dollars that buy less and less. In other words, your revenues are increasing but the payment is going nowhere; it does not get to grow.

In the static or reduced share scenario, a business earns more, again through inflated prices; the number of shares outstanding remains the same or shrinks via buyback, and the shareholder benefits by an increase in earnings per share.

Table 7.4 Inflation and Fixed Interest Payments

	This	Becomes This . . .
Gross Income	$1.00	$1.25
Fixed Interest Payments	$0.20	$0.20
Income After Interest Payment	$0.80	$1.05

Inflation Is Not Your Baby Daddy

Let us take a look at a business investment that benefits from both the earnings and fixed debt retirement features of inflation—rental property.

Inflation as It Applies to a Fourplex

In a rental property investment model, as prices increase, so do operational expenses—repairs, maintenance, insurance, and so on—but revenues (rents) can increase as well. What will not increase is the interest payment on the long-term fixed-debt mortgage.

The income statement evolves like the one shown in Table 7.5.

You can see that revenues increase proportionally at a greater rate than expenses, and yet the interest payment remains the same. Because of this, the net earnings or cash flow increases from $86 a month to $162 a month, and the cash on cash return increases from

Table 7.5   Inflation and the Rental Property Income Statement

Monthly CF Analysis	This	Becomes This . . .
Monthly Gross Rental Income	$1,275	$1,403
Minus Vacancy Loss of 8%	$102	$112
Total Income	$1,173	$1,290
Monthly Expenses		
Property Management Fee of 10%	$117	$129
Accounting	$10	$11
Insurance (Hazard)	$50	$55
Yard Work	$15	$17
Repairs and Maintenance	$90	$99
Miscellaneous	$10	$11
Reserves	$20	$22
Taxes (Property)	$100	$110
Total Expenses	$412	$454
NOI	$761	$837
Interest Payment	$675	$675
Cash Flow	$86	$162
Total Cash Put into Property	$20,750	$20,750
Cash on Cash Return	5%	9%

5 to 9 percent. When you consider that a $100,000 investment at 9 percent will grow to $236,736 over 10 years, versus $162,889 at 5 percent over the same time period, it is apparent that the benefits of inflation on rental property are significant.

Just to Drum a Point Home—Inflation as It Applies to a Public Company

At the risk of sounding like a broken record, a company with shares outstanding will realize the same effects of inflation as a fourplex owner. As prices go up, operational expenses increase, and if the business is not in a price competitive industry, revenues increase as well. (Think about Coke going from a nickel a bottle in 1950 to $1 in 2011.) In addition to long-term fixed debt, shares can remain the same or potentially decrease if the company buys them back. If the number of shares outstanding remains the same or decreases and revenues increase with inflation, earnings per share will increase. See Table 7.6.

Inflation as It Applies to a Small Business—Part Two

Typically, most small businesses do not have shares outstanding so, in most cases, the beneficial impact of inflation upon small business lies within the ability to retire fixed debt with inflated dollars. In this scenario, revenues increase, expenses increase, but the debt interest payment remains fixed.

In general, prices increase at about a rate of 4 to 6 percent a year. If a business cannot keep up with this rate, then relatively, earnings will erode as operational expenses increase without a corresponding increase in revenue.

Also keep in mind that it is wise not to have a hefty amount of debt on the balance sheet. Warren Buffett likes companies that can

Table 7.6   Inflation and the Public Company Income Statement

This . . .		Becomes This . . .	
Revenue	$100	Revenue	$150
Expenses	$50	Expenses	$75
Net Income	$50	Net Income	$75
Shares Outstanding (in Millions)	1309	Shares Outstanding (in Millions)	1080
EPS	$0.04	EPS	$0.07

retire their entire long-term debt in one to two years strictly out of earnings.

Commodity-Type Businesses

Although the ability to raise prices with inflation is a great thing for a business, the inability to raise prices is not an okay thing, it is a really bad thing. In the world of Warren Buffett, this is the place where commodity-type businesses fight to eek out a net profit. These types of businesses live within price sensitive industries where the customer couldn't care less what brand name label is slapped on the product (think aluminum, steel, and oil). What the customer does care about is the price. If Aluminum Company A is selling aluminum 20 percent cheaper than Aluminum Company B, then usually B customers will jump ship for the price.

Companies within these industries will duke it out to keep prices low and retain and attract customers. Also, many companies in these industries will have to use retained earnings to pay expenses—thus reducing plant and equipment technologies and R&D in order to effectuate new efficiencies and stay competitive, instead of launching new business ventures that would generate additional earnings at high rates of return.

Compare this to a company such as Coke, which charged $.05 a bottle in 1955 and approximately $1.00 a bottle in 2011. Over a recent 10-year period, Coke repurchased approximately 154 million shares. What this means is that, as dollar amounts have gone up in inflated revenue, expenses, and earnings, the number of shares has gone down. Thus the shareholders win, as earnings per share go up. See Table 7.7.

Table 7.7 The Beneficial Impact of Inflation

Pre-Inflation Coke Income Statement		Post-Inflation Coke Income Statement	
Revenue	$100	Revenue	$150
Expenses	$50	Expenses	$75
Net Income	$50	Net Income	$75
Shares Outstanding (in Millions)	1309	Shares Outstanding (in Millions)	1080
EPS	$0.04	EPS	$0.07

In building a business that Warren Buffett would love, it is imperative that the business has the ability to raise prices with inflation. In examining the business model, ask yourself the following questions: What were the product or service prices 10 years ago? Have they increased? If not, why not? Is it because the competition down the road undercut prices year after year? If you are starting a new business, will you have the capability to increase prices going forward? Also, does the business require large research and development and capital maintenance expenditures? See Figure 7.1 for a continuation of the road map.

Figure 7.1 Building a Small Business Warren Buffett Would Love Flowchart

With Healthy Net and Gross Margins

The key principle in seeking healthy net and gross margins, in building a business that Warren Buffett would love, is that once again, it all boils down to earnings.

Gross margin is found by dividing the gross income (revenues minus the cost of goods sold) by the total sales; both can be found on the income statement. Net margin is found by dividing the net earnings (everything left over on the income statement) by total sales dollars. The larger the number the better, and a business that has been able to deliver a healthy net margin over the years that beats both the industry average and global industry averages is a business that Warren Buffett might fall in love with.

Before You Can Have Net Margins, You Must Have Gross Margins

Let us turn once again to good old Joe and his trusty hamburger stand income statement to help illustrate the difference between gross and net margin. See Table 8.1.

We can see that after cost of goods sold (the direct labor and materials cost that goes into the product or service), Joe's $80,000 of revenue is reduced to $56,000. This is his gross income, and if we divide this number by total sales on the income statement, we get the gross margin. In this case, Joe's gross margin is 70 percent ($56,000/$80,000). This means that Joe's direct food costs and labor are taking 30 percent of revenues. By whipping out the old RMA

Table 8.1   Joe's Income Statement

Joe's Hamburger Stand		
Initial Investment	$20,000	
Revenues	$80,000	
COGs	$24,000	Gross Margin
Gross Income	$56,000	70.0%
Expenses		
Payroll	$20,000	
Payroll Taxes	$2,550	
Supplies	$1,500	
Maintenance	$2,700	
Marketing/Advertising	$1,400	
Car/Travel	$300	
Accounting and Legal	$500	
Rent	$9,600	
Phone	$900	
Utilities	$1,500	
Insurance	$1,200	
Interest	$7,000	
Depreciation	$2,500	
Total Expenses	$51,650	Net Margin
Net Income	$4,350	5.4%
Initial Rate of Return	22%	

industry common size statement from Chapter 5, we see that businesses in the restaurant industry have a cost of goods sold of 44
percent with gross margins of 56 percent. Not too shabby, Joe! You
are beating the industry by 14 percent in gross margin—this truly
is something to be proud of.

So What? What Say You, Warren?

It is fine and dandy that Joe is a superior business manager, but keep
in mind that Mr. Buffett is looking across the entire business spectrum. In other words, although Joe's hamburger stand looks great
when compared to other restaurants, Warren is looking for businesses that generate outstanding gross margin, period. A business
that consistently generates a gross margin of 80 percent, whether it
is a restaurant or not, is superior to Joe's. Cross-industry reports that

provide gross margin data similar to our ROE reports will be invaluable in analyzing for strong gross and net margin.

Gross Margin Is Really Not That Gross

Let us turn back to good old Joe and his income statement of beefy goodness in order to delve into the yin and the yang of gross margin – the net margin. See Table 8.2.

Again, It Is All about the Earnings . . . in This Case, the Net Margin

The reason that gross margin is so doggone important is that it leads to net margin, and if you start off in the income statement with a titanic cost of goods sold number leading to a svelte gross margin, then it is almost an impossibility to have a strong net margin. Net margin is merely earnings divided by sales on the income statement,

Table 8.2   Joe's Net Margin

Joe's Hamburger Stand		
Initial Investment	$20,000	
Revenues	$80,000	
COGs	$24,000	Gross Margin
Gross Income	$56,000	70.0%
Expenses		
Payroll	$20,000	
Payroll Taxes	$2,550	
Supplies	$1,500	
Maintenance	$2,700	
Marketing/Advertising	$1,400	
Car/Travel	$300	
Accounting and Legal	$500	
Rent	$9,600	
Phone	$900	
Utilities	$1,500	
Insurance	$1,200	
Interest	$7,000	
Depreciation	$2,500	
Total Expenses	$51,650	Net Margin
Net Income	$4,350	5.4%
Initial Rate of Return	22%	

and extreme emphasis has already been placed on earnings in the earlier part of the plan. If earnings are anemic, we will not have the ability to retain the earnings and grow the business; plus, our ROE will be inherently low since we are not generating much of a return.

In the end, without strong margins, we will be failing on the pillars of the Warren Buffett trifecta: strong earnings, strong return on equity, and the ability to retain earnings. Without a strong gross margin there is no strong net margin. Without net margin, inherently, earnings are weak, return is low, and the potential pile to retain is tiny at best. Thus, healthy gross margins are the first sieve to determine if net margins have a chance of being strong, and net margin is really just a second check on earnings in order to build a small business that Warren Buffett would love.

Again, Back to That Net Margin

So we see in the case of Joe's hamburger stand that $4,350 squeaks its way to the bottom line. This figure divided by gross sales gives us net margin—and now we can compare. Just as in the case of Joe's gross margin, everything is relative. In Joe's case, he is generating 5.4 percent net margin for the year ($4,350/$80,000). According to the common size industry report, restaurants are reporting a 2 percent net margin. Yikes! This is very slim. It's great that Joe is beating the industry net margin but, based on this data alone, I would be very hard pressed to start a restaurant. I would need to look at a longer track record first to make sure a healthy bottom line of earnings can be generated.

So, compared to other restaurants, Joe is doing well at a 5.4 percent net margin. This means that his operational expenses are not ravenously eating away at his gross margin, which leads to a healthy bottom line that is more than double what the industry is averaging. Now, if Joe is watering down the soup in order to make these short-term gains (or overworking his staff, or cutting corners in the kitchen, or burning himself out), this short term focus will manifest itself poorly in the financial performance of the operation. (Customers tend to spend less on watered down soup, rude, overworked waiters, and establishments whose owners have the Frigidaire logo imprinted on the side of their cheek.) Time will tell if the long-term focus is truly a short-term focus—you can only get away without putting oil in the lawn mower for so long before it breaks down. This is why it is so important to examine business on a 10-year basis and examine it on a long-term basis.

But . . .

So Joe is doing great compared to other Indians in the tribe, but how does he compare across all businesses? Remember, we are looking for strong margin/earnings here. If Joe is doubling his industry's net margin but the industry net margin is only 1 percent, Joe is still sucking wind.

Let us take a look at the net margins for various industries. See Figure 8.1.

Quite honestly, it looks like we all need to get into the beverage manufacturing business, since the net margin in this industry comes in at a whopping 17.69 percent. Coke, anyone?

Two Important Things

Keep in mind that Warren Buffett doesn't care if you are beating the industry if the industry is sucking wind as to net margins. What is the point in beating the industry margin if the industry margin is 1 percent? In order to build a small business that Warren Buffett would love, we want to make sure we have both healthy net and gross margins across the spectrum.

One other important point: As with earnings and ROE, it is imperative to check for a long-term track record. I don't care and Warren Buffett doesn't care that the business has had a 20 percent net margin this year if for the past nine years it averaged a pathetic 3 percent net margin. More than likely the future will result in a return to paltry margins. Make it a habit to track monthly the net and gross margins for your small business as found on the income statement. If you can build a consistent track record of outstanding margins, then you may have a small business that Warren Buffett loves. See Table 8.3.

And Now, a Bucketful of Consumer Monopoly Margin

What follows is a table of net and gross margin from 2011 for seven consumer monopoly companies, some of which Warren Buffett absolutely loves (Table 8.4). Although this is merely a one-year snap

	Legal Services	Healthcare	Banking	ISP	Accommodations
Revenue	100.00%	100.00%	100.00%	100.00%	100.00%
Cost of Revenue	6.78%	8.70%	8.70%	10.12%	11.13%
Gross Profit	93.22%	91.30%	91.30%	89.88%	88.87%
Officers Comp.	18.78%	1.10%	1.10%	1.68%	1.48%
Salary-Wages	28.22%	39.57%	39.57%	17.80%	23.59%
Rent	5.15%	3.86%	3.86%	3.22%	4.46%
Taxes	3.11%	5.09%	5.09%	2.21%	6.26%
Interest Paid	0.39%	2.77%	2.77%	3.01%	7.49%
Amort. & Dep.	0.86%	3.05%	3.05%	7.88%	4.57%
Advertising	2.09%	0.37%	0.37%	4.33%	2.85%
Benefits-Pension	3.42%	4.54%	4.54%	2.17%	2.60%
Other SG&A Exp.	19.03%	24.01%	24.01%	38.71%	22.64%
Total Personnel	47.00%	40.67%	40.67%	19.48%	25.07%
Total Expenses	81.04%	84.35%	84.35%	81.01%	75.95%
Net Profit	12.18%	6.95%	6.95%	8.87%	12.92%

	Accounting Services	Education	Telecommunications	Entertainment	Broadcasting
Revenue	100.00%	100.00%	100.00%	100.00%	100.00%
Cost of Revenue	12.37%	13.44%	13.49%	14.59%	19.21%
Gross Profit	87.63%	86.56%	86.51%	85.41%	80.79%
Officers Comp.	13.36%	4.90%	0.32%	11.03%	0.99%
Salary-Wages	27.92%	27.80%	12.19%	15.88%	10.97%
Rent	4.84%	6.15%	5.06%	2.84%	1.80%
Taxes	4.22%	3.24%	2.69%	2.59%	1.83%
Interest Paid	1.84%	0.81%	7.28%	1.04%	5.08%
Amort. & Dep.	1.57%	2.16%	9.46%	2.65%	13.75%
Advertising	2.69%	6.13%	1.70%	2.04%	2.99%
Benefits-Pension	3.34%	2.88%	3.17%	2.62%	3.12%
Other SG&A Exp.	18.78%	20.89%	33.66%	30.15%	32.07%
Total Personnel	41.28%	32.70%	12.50%	26.90%	11.96%
Total Expenses	78.36%	74.95%	75.52%	70.83%	72.60%
Net Profit	9.27%	11.61%	10.99%	14.58%	8.19%

	Renting/Leasing	Amusement	Publishing	TV & Audio	Computer Design
Revenue	100.00%	100.00%	100.00%	100.00%	100.00%
Cost of Revenue	19.68%	22.04%	22.96%	24.75%	28.09%
Gross Profit	80.32%	77.96%	77.04%	75.25%	71.91%
Officers Comp.	1.56%	2.85%	1.61%	3.99%	4.58%
Salary-Wages	12.58%	18.91%	21.02%	8.19%	25.12%
Rent	5.85%	5.46%	1.82%	5.03%	2.25%
Taxes	2.47%	6.29%	2.55%	1.54%	3.74%
Interest Paid	8.77%	2.94%	3.33%	11.52%	1.25%
Amort. & Dep.	19.72%	4.96%	3.98%	12.40%	2.39%
Advertising	0.79%	2.03%	3.02%	2.92%	0.52%
Benefits-Pension	1.85%	1.80%	2.76%	1.27%	2.95%
Other SG&A Exp.	15.82%	20.80%	19.75%	17.61%	20.43%
Total Personnel	14.14%	21.76%	22.63%	12.18%	29.70%
Total Expenses	69.42%	66.05%	59.83%	64.48%	63.22%
Net Profit	10.90%	11.91%	17.21%	10.77%	8.69%

Figure 8.1   Industry ROE Averages

Source: Industry Averages.com, reproduced with permission.

	Utilities	Insurance	Advertising Services	Transportation	Travel Services
Revenue	100.00%	100.00%	100.00%	100.00%	100.00%
Cost of Revenue	28.81%	29.29%	30.03%	31.94%	35.57%
Gross Profit	71.19%	70.71%	69.97%	68.06%	64.43%
Officers Comp.	1.40%	1.18%	4.46%	1.49%	2.64%
Salary-Wages	5.97%	8.83%	19.29%	17.50%	13.29%
Rent	1.35%	2.28%	3.61%	5.98%	1.77%
Taxes	7.19%	1.40%	2.18%	3.67%	2.05%
Interest Paid	10.86%	15.80%	2.72%	0.95%	1.94%
Amort. & Dep.	13.89%	1.47%	2.10%	4.10%	1.85%
Advertising	0.25%	0.55%	3.59%	0.24%	4.33%
Benefits-Pension	3.73%	1.23%	1.72%	3.11%	1.61%
Other SG&A Exp.	17.65%	20.11%	22.58%	26.50%	22.06%
Total Personnel	7.37%	10.00%	23.74%	19.00%	15.93%
Total Expenses	62.29%	52.84%	62.24%	63.53%	51.53%
Net Profit	8.90%	17.87%	7.73%	4.53%	12.90%

	Research/Devel.	Food Services	Waste Management	Engineering Services	Beverage Manuf.
Revenue	100.00%	100.00%	100.00%	100.00%	100.00%
Cost of Revenue	36.30%	37.70%	39.17%	40.08%	42.91%
Gross Profit	63.70%	62.30%	60.83%	59.92%	57.09%
Officers Comp.	3.01%	2.07%	1.70%	6.87%	0.52%
Salary-Wages	16.71%	18.90%	13.92%	19.20%	8.05%
Rent	2.85%	6.52%	2.66%	3.05%	0.79%
Taxes	2.46%	3.86%	3.79%	2.82%	7.23%
Interest Paid	1.69%	1.54%	4.46%	0.61%	3.49%
Amort. & Dep.	2.86%	2.51%	6.44%	1.32%	3.14%
Advertising	0.56%	2.35%	0.34%	0.34%	3.95%
Benefits-Pension	2.71%	1.36%	2.28%	3.55%	2.44%
Other SG&A Exp.	19.20%	15.09%	17.54%	15.67%	9.79%
Total Personnel	19.72%	20.98%	15.62%	26.07%	8.57%
Total Expenses	52.05%	54.22%	53.13%	53.43%	39.40%
Net Profit	11.65%	8.08%	7.70%	6.49%	17.69%

	Agricultural	Oil/Gas Extraction	Clothing Stores	Staffing Services	Outdoor Activities
Revenue	100.00%	100.00%	100.00%	100.00%	100.00%
Cost of Revenue	43.77%	44.24%	51.54%	55.02%	56.72%
Gross Profit	56.23%	55.76%	48.46%	44.98%	43.28%
Officers Comp.	1.83%	0.95%	1.48%	1.79%	2.76%
Salary-Wages	7.06%	3.16%	13.61%	22.61%	7.09%
Rent	5.80%	0.85%	7.04%	0.93%	2.46%
Taxes	1.93%	2.88%	2.22%	6.07%	1.85%
Interest Paid	1.96%	2.99%	0.74%	0.41%	1.01%
Amort. & Dep.	4.51%	5.52%	2.03%	0.49%	2.77%
Advertising	0.45%	0.03%	2.48%	0.35%	0.46%
Benefits-Pension	1.14%	0.66%	1.34%	3.31%	0.75%
Other SG&A Exp.	21.62%	13.86%	9.55%	5.98%	16.18%
Total Personnel	8.88%	4.11%	15.09%	24.40%	9.84%
Total Expenses	46.29%	30.69%	40.48%	41.94%	35.33%
Net Profit	9.94%	25.07%	7.98%	3.04%	7.95%

Figure 8.1   (Continued)

	Power Generation	Home Store	Clothing Manuf.	Forest/Logging	Food Manufacturing
Revenue	100.00%	100.00%	100.00%	100.00%	100.00%
Cost of Revenue	56.75%	57.11%	61.58%	61.89%	62.60%
Gross Profit	43.25%	42.89%	38.42%	38.11%	37.40%
Officers Comp.	0.30%	2.12%	2.08%	1.65%	0.58%
Salary-Wages	3.78%	12.57%	8.83%	5.87%	4.78%
Rent	1.94%	4.78%	2.18%	1.42%	1.34%
Taxes	3.24%	2.23%	1.95%	1.81%	2.00%
Interest Paid	6.18%	0.53%	1.25%	2.25%	2.42%
Amort. & Dep.	6.56%	1.29%	1.28%	3.99%	2.07%
Advertising	0.09%	4.54%	2.22%	0.16%	2.87%
Benefits-Pension	1.96%	1.10%	1.42%	0.74%	1.89%
Other SG&A Exp.	14.03%	9.17%	10.09%	12.25%	8.01%
Total Personnel	4.08%	14.69%	10.91%	7.52%	5.36%
Total Expenses	38.07%	38.31%	31.30%	30.14%	25.97%
Net Profit	5.18%	4.58%	7.12%	7.97%	11.43%

	Hardware Store	Trade Contractors	Equipment Manuf.	Electronics Store	General Stores
Revenue	100.00%	100.00%	100.00%	100.00%	100.00%
Cost of Revenue	63.66%	65.86%	68.02%	69.24%	69.33%
Gross Profit	36.34%	34.14%	31.98%	30.76%	30.67%
Officers Comp.	2.94%	4.10%	0.28%	1.43%	0.13%
Salary-Wages	12.29%	7.23%	4.44%	10.26%	10.85%
Rent	2.96%	2.06%	2.77%	2.32%	2.19%
Taxes	2.13%	2.25%	0.99%	1.63%	1.73%
Interest Paid	0.63%	0.46%	3.32%	0.49%	1.00%
Amort. & Dep.	1.23%	1.52%	4.24%	0.85%	1.44%
Advertising	1.52%	0.37%	1.03%	2.22%	1.45%
Benefits-Pension	1.29%	1.84%	2.73%	0.70%	1.28%
Other SG&A Exp.	6.89%	8.36%	5.38%	6.18%	5.70%
Total Personnel	15.23%	11.33%	4.72%	11.69%	10.98%
Total Expenses	31.89%	28.20%	25.17%	26.08%	25.76%
Net Profit	4.45%	5.94%	6.81%	4.68%	4.91%

	Engineering Constr.	Wood Manuf.	Food/Bev Store	Building Construction	Wholesale Trade
Revenue	100.00%	100.00%	100.00%	100.00%	100.00%
Cost of Revenue	70.01%	70.92%	71.68%	77.18%	77.30%
Gross Profit	29.99%	29.08%	28.32%	22.82%	22.70%
Officers Comp.	2.11%	1.83%	0.51%	1.73%	1.36%
Salary-Wages	4.24%	5.79%	9.91%	3.39%	6.01%
Rent	2.18%	0.97%	2.02%	0.74%	1.09%
Taxes	1.65%	1.56%	1.60%	1.05%	0.91%
Interest Paid	1.01%	2.31%	0.85%	0.69%	0.74%
Amort. & Dep.	2.34%	2.12%	1.47%	0.48%	1.50%
Advertising	0.19%	0.55%	0.63%	0.31%	1.07%
Benefits-Pension	1.20%	1.55%	1.84%	0.65%	0.85%
Other SG&A Exp.	6.23%	5.45%	6.48%	6.30%	4.93%
Total Personnel	6.36%	7.62%	10.42%	5.12%	7.37%
Total Expenses	21.15%	22.13%	25.32%	15.33%	18.45%
Net Profit	8.84%	6.95%	3.00%	7.49%	4.25%

	Car Dealers	Gas Station
Revenue	100.00%	100.00%
Cost of Revenue	85.60%	88.22%
Gross Profit	14.40%	11.78%
Officers Comp.	0.69%	0.40%
Salary-Wages	5.03%	3.12%
Rent	0.94%	0.96%
Taxes	0.81%	1.04%
Interest Paid	0.63%	0.42%
Amort. & Dep.	0.39%	0.94%
Advertising	1.07%	0.11%
Benefits-Pension	0.47%	0.23%
Other SG&A Exp.	2.74%	2.89%
Total Personnel	5.72%	3.52%
Total Expenses	12.76%	10.10%
Net Profit	1.64%	1.68%

Figure 8.1 (Continued)

164

Table 8.3   A Healthy Gross and Net Margin

Joe's Hamburger Stand

Initial Investment	$20,000	
Revenues	$80,000	
COGs	$24,000	Gross Margin
Gross Income	$56,000	70.0%
Expenses		
Payroll	$20,000	
Payroll Taxes	$2,550	
Supplies	$1,500	
Maintenance	$2,700	
Marketing/Advertising	$1,400	
Car/Travel	$300	
Accounting and Legal	$500	
Rent	$9,600	
Phone	$900	
Utilities	$1,500	
Insurance	$1,200	
Interest	$7,000	
Depreciation	$2,500	
Total Expenses	$51,650	Net Margin
Net Income	$4,350	5.4%
Initial Rate of Return	22%	

Table 8.4   Consumer Monopoly Margin

	2011	
	Gross Margin	Net Margin
Coke	63.9%	34.0%
McDonald's	40.0%	20.6%
Wal-Mart	22.6%	3.9%
Disney	17.7%	10.4%
Kellogg's	42.7%	10.1%
Campbell's	41.0%	11.0%
Hershey's	42.6%	9.0%

Source: Morningstar.com.

shot and I strongly advise you to analyze margin over a 10-year track record, this is how the big boys do it, and it is very telling of what a strong margin looks like. This is the best of the best. Check out the Coke and McDonald's margins: 63.9, 34, 40, and 20.6 percent respectively. Outstanding!

Figure 8.2 continues to detail the road map we've been following!

Figure 8.2   Building a Small Business Warren Buffett Would Love the Flowchart

CHAPTER 9

Building a Small Business That Warren Buffett Would Love— Finishing the Landscape

The Spirit

Put down your paintbrushes, take a step back, and observe the landscape we have just painted.

I Want to See a Consumer Monopoly . . .

A small business that Warren Buffett loves must take up retail space within the hearts and minds of consumers. For a small business owner, it is imperative to build a strong brand that is distinctive and different from the competition, otherwise consumers will just go across the street once the other guy lowers his gas prices. Remember, the core of a strong business is not a mystery nor is it a complicated mess. It is found in the wisdom of Warren Buffett, and it is found in the types of companies that he loves.

Folks have to have it: T-shirts.

A brand, not a commodity: Fruit of the Loom.

Folks have to have it: Food, soup, McNuggets, Snap, Crackle, Pop.

A brand, not a commodity: McDonald's, Campbell's, Kellogg's, Hershey's.

Folks have to have it: Liquids, water, juice, soda pop.

A brand, not a commodity: Coke, Pepsi, and . . . Coke.

Folks have to have it: The happiest place on earth.

A brand, not a commodity: Disney.

With a Strong Track Record of Earnings . . .

Past performance is not necessarily a guaranteed indicator of future results, but when it comes to building a small business that Warren Buffett loves, a track record of consistent and growing earnings is priceless. The small business with a hearty record of earnings is likely to continue producing robust earnings. Find the income statement, become its friend, hug it, love it, view it over a 10-year period. (See Table 9.1.)

A Healthy Return on Equity . . .

A business is only as good as its return. If the investor down the street is generating a higher return, then it is time to manage the business for operational efficiencies, or it is time to see if the guy down the street needs a partner. (See Table 9.2.)

With the Ability to Reinvest Those Earnings at a High Rate of Return . . .

If you can build an economic powerhouse, a small business engine generating high returns that Warren Buffett loves, then you should reinvest the earnings back into this Corvette. You do not own a jalopy, and if you in fact own a vehicle that can perform at a high level, then why would you not put fuel back into it? (See Table 9.3.)

Table 9.1   Consumer Monopoly Earnings Per Share

	McDonald's	Coke	Disney	Kellogg's	Hershey's	Campbell's	Wal-Mart
2001	$1.25	$1.60	$(0.02)	$1.16	$0.75	$1.55	$1.49
2002	$0.70	$1.23	$0.61	$1.75	$1.47	$1.28	$1.49
2003	$1.15	$1.77	$0.62	$1.92	$1.73	$1.45	$1.81
2004	$1.79	$2.00	$1.12	$2.14	$2.30	$1.57	$2.07
2005	$2.04	$2.04	$1.22	$2.36	$1.99	$1.71	$2.41
2006	$2.83	$2.16	$1.64	$2.51	$2.34	$1.85	$2.68
2007	$1.98	$2.57	$2.25	$2.76	$0.93	$2.16	$2.71
2008	$3.76	$2.49	$2.28	$2.99	$1.36	$3.06	$3.13
2009	$4.11	$2.93	$1.76	$3.16	$1.90	$2.06	$3.39
2010	$4.58	$5.06	$2.03	$3.30	$2.21	$2.42	$3.70

Source: Morningstar.com.

Table 9.2 Consumer Monopoly Return on Equity

	McDonald's	Coke	Disney	Kellogg's	Hershey's	Campbell's	Wal-Mart
2001	17.51%	38.38%	0.68%	53.54%	17.84%	—	20.08%
2002	9.04%	26.33%	5.36%	81.61%	32.04%	—	21.60%
2003	13.22%	33.58%	5.36%	67.32%	34.51%	435.90%	21.83%
2004	17.40%	32.29%	9.40%	48.14%	49.88%	102.62%	22.08%
2005	17.73%	30.18%	9.69%	43.18%	46.74%	65.95%	21.90%
2006	23.16%	30.53%	11.63%	46.14%	65.65%	50.43%	19.67%
2007	15.58%	30.94%	14.98%	48.01%	33.56%	55.76%	20.18%
2008	30.01%	27.51%	14.04%	57.78%	68.36%	89.17%	20.63%
2009	33.20%	30.15%	10.01%	65.16%	83.95%	71.96%	21.08%
2010	34.51%	42.32%	11.12%	56.30%	62.83%	102.06%	23.53%
Average ROE	**21.14%**	**32.22%**	**9.23%**	**56.72%**	**49.54%**	**97.38%**	**21.26%**

Source: Morningstar.com.

Table 9.3 Retained Earnings

In(millions)	McDonald's	Coke	Disney	Kellogg's	Hershey's	Campbell's	Wal-Mart
	2010 Retained Earnings to Sales						
RE	$33,812	$49,278	$34,327	$6,122	$4,375	$8,760	$66,638
Sales	$24,075	$35,119	$38,063	$12,397	$5,671	$7,676	$421,849
RE/Sales	1.40%	1.40%	0.90%	0.49%	0.77%	1.14%	0.16%

Source: Morningstar.com.

With Little or No Debt on the Balance Sheet . . .

Debt can be part of a good capital fuel mixture for a business, but too much of it and the interest payments will start socking you in the earnings ribs. Companies with true consumer brand equity have tons of cash lying around and thus have little need for hefty amounts of debt. (They have to shove the excess cash somewhere!) Thus, a business that Warren Buffett loves has the ability to pay off long-term debt in one to two years using earnings. (See Table 9.4.)

The Ability to Increase Prices with Inflation . . .

Although we all long for the days when a Coke cost a nickel, a ticket to Disney cost $3.50, and a box of Kellogg's Corn Flakes cost 10 cents, the fact is that these prices will not return (see Table 9.5). Instead they will continue to rise as long as excess dollars are printed, production costs continue to increase, and international borrowing and lending continues. Companies with long-term fixed debt, a static or decreasing number of stock shares, and the ability to increase prices with inflation will be the ones who have the ability to crest this wave and ride it like a surfer banshee out of hell.

And a Healthy Net and Gross Margin Relative to Other Businesses and Industries

It's all about the Benjamins. In this case it's all about the Benjamins that are found after cost of goods sold has been removed (gross margin) and after all other expenses have had their meal (net margin). Businesses with anemic bottom lines also inherently generate paltry, sad returns. A business with good margins and return on equity is a small business that Warren Buffett would love. (See Table 9.6.)

Finis! A Landscape Framed

You stand before a beautiful, rich landscape, one that Warren Buffett would love. This landscape has been painted time and again on the canvases of the world's greatest businesses: Coke, Hershey's, McDonald's, Campbell's, Kellogg's, Fruit of the Loom. Now, the lights are dimming, the murmurs of the crowd are stifling to a hush, the curtain is being drawn. It is your turn to take the stage. You are on.

Table 9.4 Low Debt Levels

(in millions)	McDonald's	Coke	Disney	Kellogg's	Hershey's	Campbell's	Wal-Mart
Total LTD	$14,416	$23,410	$20,687	$6,505	$2,072	$3,285	$53,637
Current Net Earnings	$4,946	$11,809	$3,963	$1,247	$510	$844	$16,389
Debt/Earnings or # of Years to Pay off (two or less is Buffett-licious!)	2.91	1.98	5.22	5.22	4.06	3.89	3.27

Source: Morningstar.com.

Table 9.5   The Benefits of Inflation

Price of a McDonald's Hamburger		Price of a Coke		Price of a Ticket to Disney World	
1955	$0.15	1950	$0.05	1971	$3.50
2011	$0.95	2011	$1.00	2010	$80.00

Table 9.6   Healthy Gross and Net Margins

	2011	
	Gross Margin	Net Margin
Coke	63.9%	34.0%
McDonald's	40.0%	20.6%
Wal-Mart	22.6%	3.9%
Disney	17.7%	10.4%
Kellogg's	42.7%	10.1%
Campbell's	41.0%	11.0%
Hershey's	42.6%	9.0%

Source: Morningstar.com.

You are the master painter and should revel in the confidence that you have a painter's toolbox chock full of powerful tools that can be leveraged to build a small business that Warren Buffett would love. Do not be afraid or ashamed to pick up the palette, paints, and brushes that have been laid at your feet, adjust your canvas, and put on some mood music, perhaps some Liza Minnelli or Metallica. Start painting up in that little left corner, slowly at first, perhaps a little orange will go good there. Do not be afraid to take some broader brush strokes, perhaps a solid line of black earnings at the bottom, some purple return on equity in the forefront. Paint in from the right, perhaps some blue, a yellow sun, and a lush green thicket of inflating trees nesting cozily in the belly of a great mountain of brand loyalty. A winding dirt path snakes lazily between a patch of evergreen return on equity, on its way into an unknown adventure involving little debt. The music swells, your heart races. With Warren Buffett's hand resting on top of yours, you are painting a beautiful landscape, one that Warren Buffett himself smiles at and loves.

Epilogue

The Business Plan—Well, Yeah, There Is an Outline, but This Is Not *War and Peace*

If you perform a web search on the term "business plan outline" or peruse your local book warehouse, you will inevitably come across half a dozen varying outlines. My motto is: Find one that you are comfortable with and then get very comfortable with that outline. Whether you are dusting off the old business plan or starting from scratch, you need to familiarize yourself with a good outline. And remember, this is not *War and Peace.*

Here is the one I use:

Executive Summary

The Business
  Vision and Mission
      Strengths and Weaknesses
      Legal Structure
      Business Description
      Product or Service Description
      IP Property Description
      Location
      Management Personnel
      Records
      Insurance
      Security

A Living, Breathing, Implementable Document

In a perfect world, your business plan would sprout arms and operate the cash register, but the truth is, it is probably dead in a drawer somewhere next to an old Kenny Rogers CD that you keep around for "me" time. Your mission is to find that drawer, open drawer, grab feather duster, and get to work. Your business plan contains your hopes and dreams for the business as well as how to operate the whole thing. It sure as heck deserves a better fate than Kenny.

As far as the living, breathing, and implementing part, your business plan should be wired into your business. At a minimum, this is accomplished by reviewing and tracking the key elements of the plan at biweekly and quarterly meetings. According to Dr. Matt

Marvel, Professor of Entrepreneurship at Western Kentucky University, "The bane of most entrepreneurs is the lack of business plan implementation. For the most part, business owners find it difficult to integrate the plan into the business. This is a critical failure point for most small businesses."

Let's examine specific sections and see how you are stacking up.

The Vision and Mission

Sometimes viewed as the enlightening, blue-sky statement that hangs on the manager's wood paneling wall, your mission statement sounds idealistic and cute but typically runs into a brick wall called reality. The real world says to hell with the idyllic view of how the business should run—I'm in charge. The mission statement, though, is the reason why you went into business in the first place. The vision and mission, at a minimum, are the driving forces of the business. They serve as the fountainhead used to slog through the daily onslaught of reality and should be kept in the forefront and reviewed daily. If the overall mission or vision for the business has not been developed, then stop now, do not pass go, do not collect $200. Get to work putting a solid mission statement together by asking yourself, "Who do we serve, why do we serve them, and how do we serve them?" What is the overall purpose for being in business? What should the business look like now and in the future? Write your statement down and read it out loud at every meeting.

Business Description and Product or Service Description

This section typically states: "We will deliver quality service and products in a unique and outstanding environment. Our customers will be wowed by us until their heads explode." Great! Now the question is, how is this glorious statement going to impact the business? What is the standard for following up on customer satisfaction and product quality? Do you survey the customer on a regular basis, bring up the results in team meetings, and powwow on solutions to the situation? You should be.

This brings us to our next area of planning and integration.

Management and Personnel

If you bring your A game to this section, an organizational chart will be developed. If you bring your A game, a cup of coffee, and a knack for delegating, then roles, responsibilities, and accountability for each position will be fleshed out in the organizational chart. In keeping with the previous product and service example, if no one at a team meeting knows who is responsible for improving customer service, then chances are good that the business has some unhappy customers. If the organizational chart indicates that Joe Bob is responsible for customer satisfaction, the meeting script would go something like this: "Joe, we are receiving a fair amount of customer complaints. Any insight into why this is happening?"

Joe would ideally wake up from his afternoon nap and ask, "Are you talking to me?"

On a serious note, this process will allow management to follow up on individual responsibilities and enforce accountability. If everyone knows their roles and responsibilities, they can focus their efforts.

Marketing

The marketing section typically details the varying channels that will be employed to market the business—web, print, radio, blimps, wacky-waving-inflatable-arm-flailing tube men, and so on. It should also include a method of grading the effectiveness of each channel. If the newspaper ads are providing a rate of return of 150 percent but the radio spots are barely breaking even, perhaps it is time to kick the radio channel and beef up the print ads.

Finally, Financials

No matter how you slice it, the health of the business always boils down to the money. Budgets should be prepared on a monthly basis and need to be reconciled back to actuals. If this is not in the works, then, once more, do not pass go, do not collect $200, go directly to your local book warehouse and find a book on budgeting. This is a very important procedure. A financial forecast was developed as part of the business plan. This forecast needs to be revisited since it may turn up opportunities for improvement.

It is also important to be familiar with the balance sheet and cash flow statements. Ideally, the business is increasing in equity over time, not metastasizing into a raging spiral of death. If you find yourself constantly throwing good money after bad, it is time for radical improvement or for cutting the losses.

Goals and Milestones—You Said You Were Going to Live Up to Them, How Did You Do?

Although by all appearances *The Secret* was a profitable attempt to repackage motivational material from the 1980s and market it into an international bestselling book and DVD, the real secret lies in setting meaningful goals and milestones for the business and keeping them in the forefront at all times. Goals will serve as the engine that drives the entrepreneurial spirit even when you don't want to go into work in the morning. Goals will provide direction for the company and prompt action steps to move closer toward the end game.

Goals

A goal is a deadline that you set for yourself in order to reach an outcome that you strongly, personally desire. It is a dream with a deadline attached, and thus you can make it a 10-yard pass, a 50-yard pass, or a 100-yard pass. If you've always wanted to write a book, then set a goal and write a book. If you've wanted to build a website, build a website. Run a marathon? Do it. Live on an exotic island in the Caribbean? Make a plan and stick with it. In this section I will detail how to do this, providing you with the opportunity to set a financial independence goal and work towards it.

Traditionally, goals have been seen as metrics that either athletes or salesman set for themselves in order to judge their performance. In high school it might have been the track star's miles per minute goal, or in the real world it might have been Joe Insurance's policy that he sold you. In truth, a goal metric is something that can belong to you. It's your road map to get something that you strongly desire, and it doesn't have to always be grandiose or materialistic— perhaps you just want to call your mom once a week—go for it.

What follows are the details on how to set goals, how to keep them in the forefront of your daily life, and how to keep your persistence levels high throughout the process.

Our Goal-Setting Toolbox

- Write it down.
- Be specific.
- Create 10-yard and 50-yard plays.

- Keep it in a place where you can see it.
- Read it three times a day.
- Rewrite your goals a couple of times a day.
- Visualize as complete.
- Affirm it out loud in the present tense.
- Track it—if you can measure it, you can reach it.
- Victory log.
- Plan the night before.
- Vision boards.
- The question.

Step 1: Write It Out   First, you need to determine the picture of your ideal day. Where do you see yourself in five years? What would you consider a stretch for you in your career, financially and personally? What kind of career success will you have, how much money? What does your family life look like?

Below are some category suggestions you might use as your overall framework for goal setting.

1. Happiness
2. Family and friends
3. Finance
4. Career
5. Health
6. Hobbies
7. House (mowing the lawn always makes its way onto the list)
8. Service

Think about each of these areas. What's the ultimate picture you develop regarding where you will be three to five years down the road? In developing this picture, set some higher benchmarks, 50-yard passes, as well as lower benchmarks, 10-yard passes. Once you have this picture it is time to write it down. Ideally, you should shoot for 10 decent goals that will push you toward the ideal picture that you have developed. Shoot for a list of 100 if you desire; the sky is the limit.

Now it is time to bring that picture into reality, write it down, and keep it in a spot where you can review it two to three times a day. The main elements of a written goal are that it has a timeline and a specific description—it's a dream with a deadline. Thus, if you want to lose weight it's much less effective to say "I want to be slimmer" than it is to say "I want to weigh 170 pounds by September 22, 2009, at 7 P.M." In the second example you have a specific date and even a time, 7 P.M. Be as specific as possible. In this version, you've stated how much you are going to weigh: 170 pounds. It will be easy to jump on the scale on September 22, 2009, at 7 P.M. and see if in fact you weigh 170.

If you want a new car, describe in detail the make, model, and color and perhaps all the features of the car. Go to your favorite car's showroom, take a picture of yourself behind the wheel, and post it on your bulletin board. If you want a vacation home on an exotic beach, describe what it looks like and the sights and sounds you see as you sit on the beach in front of the bungalow. Write it down and be as specific as possible.

In addition to this, you need to put your goal in the present tense and write it in an affirming sense as if you have already achieved it. "I am thoroughly enjoying being in great shape, weighing 170 pounds by September 22, 2009, at 7 P.M. I feel healthy and great."

These action verbs and the feeling of present tense will help your mind close the gap faster by bringing the goal into reality.

Write down your top 10—put them in a notebook, on your computer, or on note cards and review them daily.

Step 2: Read It Two to Three Times a Day   Now that you have your list, you need to put some daily action behind it. Read it to yourself two to three times a day, out loud if the opportunity presents itself. Be diligent about this. It should be like brushing your teeth. Read the goals in the morning and before going to bed. This one action could take up to 10 minutes a day while putting you in the top 10 percent of all achievers.

Step 3: Now Visualize It   Continue on with the daydreaming from the initial setup that spurred your goals list. At least twice a day spend 5 to 10 minutes visualizing your written goals as already complete. What does it feel like to drive that 1965 white Mustang, breezing down a country road? What sights and sounds do you see and hear? How does the wind feel blowing through your hair? What tunes do you have playing on the radio? Who is by your side in the seat next to you—your wife or the dog?

For that vacation home on the beach—what do the waves feel like as they lap against your feet? How warm is the water? Do you hear laid-back Hawaiian music playing or merely the roar of the ocean? Can you smell coconut or the sun tan lotion? Do you have a beach bungalow or a beach mansion? Can you hear the seagulls baying in the distance?

Scientists claim that the mind does not know the difference between repeated visualization and reality. In the end what you are trying to do is program yourself to look for the opportunities to move towards your goals on a daily basis. When you visualize your goals daily as already complete, your mind will strive to close the gap between reality and your daydream.

Step 4: Affirm It Out Loud   Okay, I don't want people to think you are crazy, but if you can find a nice quiet place where preferably you are alone, you should read your goals out loud at least twice a day. This is reinforcing even further that you are closer to the reality of your goal. Affirm it out loud in the present tense—read what you have written—"I am thoroughly enjoying having a net worth of $1 million by October 31st, 2009, at 7 P.M. This money brings great joy to my life and gives me the freedom to travel the world."

Read it out loud.

Step 5: Rewrite It   Also, if you have time, rewrite your top 10 goals at least once a day. I'm not saying spend all of your time working on these techniques instead of actually following through on the goals, but be diligent about these tactics and at the most, for your top 10, all of the steps laid out before should take no more than a total of 30 minutes a day, and the rewards from the time invested will be well worth it.

Rewrite the top 10—keep your dreams in the forefront of your daily activities.

End

Don't be afraid to dream big; don't be afraid to believe in yourself, and remember, lob some 50-yard passes right along with the 10-yard passes. Experiment with a mix of incremental steps and giant leaps. The net, net is to build the life that you are most interested in living.

Be diligent, follow through on these steps, and achievement and progress will be a constant factor in your life.

In the existing business plan, the goals should be reviewed and measured in order to judge how much progress has been made. If not, then the question is, why not? Keep the business goals in front of you and your staff at all times and remember to be specific. It is much better to say "I want to weigh 171 by December 25, 2011, at 7 P.M." than "I want to lose weight." In the second example you can take off a sock and cheer "mission accomplished." In the first example you have to step on a scale on December 25 and face the facts.

Some goals and milestones you may want to think about:

1. Exit Strategy—An exit strategy is not a planned fire escape route. It is the ultimate goal for the business. Will you work until you hit the ripe old age of 110, hand it off to the kids, or sell it for a nice sum of cash? Michael Gerber, author of *The e-Myth Revisited,* asserts that the goal of every business owner is to eventually sell the business. How much will you sell it for?

2. Financial Independence—When will you be financially independent? At what point will your passive income be equal to or greater than your expenses?

3. Revenues—What will sales levels look like in the next three to five years?

4. Expansion—Do you wish to expand and open additional stores this year, create a new strategic alliance, or perhaps diversify your product offerings? Remember to be discriminating with your time. Many business opportunities will come your way and it is best to be selective and focused.

Implementation—It's a Pretty Document . . . So What?

As I mentioned, if you have a great plan chock full of financially literate terms such as "nominal rate of return" and "net present value," then good for you—you have a great vocabulary. If you actually wire the plan into the business, then you have the start of a solid business model in addition to a great vocabulary. I can't emphasis this enough: The plan needs to be integrated into the business on a strategic and tactical level via company meetings and day-to-day operations. The individuals responsible for facilitating the key functions of the business need their roles and responsibilities to be spelled out, including an accountability standard. The mission, vision, and goals should be at the forefront of the business. The cash flow projection should be reviewed monthly.

In summary, the business plan is typically gathering dust in a drawer next to a fork stashed away for lunch. More than likely, the initial development process was haphazard, painstaking, and a relief to finish. In reality the plan, if done correctly, implemented, and reviewed, can provide a great vision and map for the business to succeed. It provides a standard of operation and delivers a consistent value proposition to the customers. It creates the future by laying out goals and milestones, and builds railroad tracks to reach the destination. It is a cliché to say it is a "living document," but it is true that the business plan can be a multi-cylindered engine that drives you to a better business model.

Notes

Introduction: Painting the Picture of the Ideal Business

1. Mary Buffett, Mary and David Clark, *Buffettology* (New York: Fireside, 1999), 24–25.
2. Alice Schroeder, *The Snowball* (New York: Bantam, 2008).
3. *Domino's Income Statement*. Retrieved July 23, 2011, from http://financials.morningstar.com/income-statement/is .html?t=DPZ&region=USA&culture=en-US.

Chapter 1: Buffett and the Fundamental Business Perspective

1. Mark Pendergrast, *For God, Country and Coca-Cola*, 2nd ed. (New York: Basic Books, 2000).
2. *Coca-Cola's Income Statement*. Retrieved April 17, 2011, from http://financials .morningstar.com/income-statement/is.html?t=KO.
3. *Coca-Cola's Financial Statements*. Retrieved May 3, 2011, from http://financials .morningstar.com/income-statement/is.html?t=KO.
4. *Food Timeline*. Retrieved May 3, 2011, from www.foodtimeline.org/foodfaq5 .html.
5. *Risk-Free T-Bills*. Retrieved July 15, 2011, from www.treasury.gov/resource-center/ data-chart-center/interest-rates/Pages/TextView.aspx?data=billrates.
6. Mary Buffett, and David Clark, *Buffettology* (New York: Fireside, 1999), 41.
7. Ibid., 35.

Chapter 2: The Importance of a Consumer Monopoly or Toll Bridge

1. *Gerber company info*. Retrieved May 30, 2011, from www.gerber.com/AllStages/ About/Heritage.aspxgerber.com.

2. *Nestle Brands.* Retrieved June 1, 2011, from www.nestle.com/Brands/Pages/ Brands.aspxnestle.com.
3. *Number of Domino's Franchises.* Retrieved June 1, 2011, from www.dominosbiz .com/Biz-Public-EN/Site+Content/Secondary/Franchise/dominos.com.
4. Steve LeFever, *Profit Mastery* (Seattle: Business Resource Services, 2008), 31.
5. Ibid., 32.
6. *McDonald's Revenue Data.* Retrieved July 15, 2011, from http://quote.morningstar .com/stock/s.aspx?t=mcd–morningstar.com.
7. Bill Chiaravalle and Barbara Findlay Schenck, *Branding For Dummies* (Hoboken, NJ: John Wiley & Sons, 2006).

Chapter 3: Strong, Consistent, and Growing Earnings

1. Mary Buffett and David Clark, *Buffettology* (New York: Fireside, 1999), 35.
2. Forty-first President of the United States stumping on the subject of education in the state of South Carolina.
3. Mary Buffett and David Clark, *The Tao of Warren Buffett* (New York: Scribner, 2006).
4. Steve LeFever, *Profit Mastery* (Seattle: Business Resource Services, 2008).
5. Buffett and Clark, *Buffettology*, 102.
6. *McDonald's Revenue Data.* Retrieved July 15, 2011, from http://quote.morningstar .com/stock/s.aspx?t=mcd– morningstar.com.
7. Fred R. Shapiro and Joseph Epstein, *The Yale Book of Quotations* (New Haven: Yale University Press, 2006).
8. *McDonaldland Mascots.* Retrieved June 30, 2011, from http://able2know.org/ topic/169266-1-able2know.org.

Chapter 4: Emphasizing a High Return on Equity

1. Mary Buffett and David Clark, *Buffettology* (New York: Fireside, 1999), 104–105.
2. Alice Schroeder, *The Snowball* (New York: Bantam, 2008).
3. Robert T. Kiyosaki, *Rich Dad, Poor Dad* (Scottsdale, AZ: TechPress, 2002).
4. Buffett and Clark, *Buffettology*, 166.

Chapter 5: Retained Earnings—The Fuel for the Engine of Compounding Returns

1. Alice Schroeder, *The Snowball* (New York: Bantam, 2008).
2. *Coke Brands.* Retrieved July 15, 2011, from www.worldofcoca-cola.com/?WT .cl=1&WT.mm=top-left-menu11-worldofcoke-red_en_UScoca-cola.com.

Chapter 6: The Tumor of Long-Term Debt

1. Warren Buffett likes companies that can pay off their debts in one to two years out of earnings; see *Buffettology*.

2. Peter Lynch, *One Up on Wall Street* (New York, Simon & Schuster, 2000). (Companies with 33 percent D/E.)
3. Ten Advantages of Real Estate; see *Rich Dad, Poor Dad.*

Chapter 7: Keeping Up with the Joneses

1. *Disney ticket inflation data.* Retrieved August 3, 2011, from www.foodtimeline.org/foodfaq5.html.

About the Author

Adam Brownlee is the author of four books on the subjects of business and investing: *My Happy Assets, Small Business Coffee Hour, Taking the Last Steps to Financial Independence* and the soon to be published, *Building a Small Business That Abraham Lincoln Would Love.* As the Director of the Small Business Development Center at Western Kentucky University, he consulted with hundreds of small business owners in the areas of financial management, accounting, strategic management, financial analysis, business plan development and web and marketing strategies. In the past he has served as a computer programmer and currently teaches courses on business, finance, and investing while serving as a business analyst to one of the nation's leading online retailers, www.campingworld.com.

He lives in the Bowling Green, Kentucky, area with his wife Michelle and space-ranger kid, Cooper.

Index